The

Spiritual Awakening

of an

Analytical Mind

*13 Stepping-Stones to Help
Guide Your Journey*

Tina L. Moody

The Spiritual Awakening of an Analytical Mind
Copyright © 2021 Tina L. Moody

ISBN: 978-1-63381-275-8

Designed and produced by:
Maine Authors Publishing
12 High Street, Thomaston, Maine
www.maineauthorspublishing.com

Printed in the United States of America

To Sam and Cooper, my greatest teachers.
What you will create in your lives is beyond my imagination.
I love you and am so proud of you.

Author Declaration

I am not a counselor or a licensed practitioner, nor do I follow any particular belief system. I am simply an analytical thinker of mainstream America who has recently awakened to the gifts of the intuitive mind. I have been guided to help build a bridge between these two ways of being as we feel the shift in the universal energy of a raised consciousness. This book is a bridge for my fellow analytical thinkers.

Contents

Introduction

Welcome! No need to feel uncomfortable or overwhelmed. I am one of you. As a fellow analytical with linear thinking, I am here as a facilitator to help guide you through some stepping-stones that will allow you to begin to open to all our Universe has to offer.

Before we really dig into things, I want to be up-front and tell you that you are embarking on a self-awakening journey. The fact you are sitting with book in hand tells me this. I hesitate to call it a "spiritual awakening" as not to scare you away. In fact, call it what you feel comfortable in calling it. Working on yourself. Reprioritizing what is important in your life. In search of something bigger. Call it spiritual if you have made peace with the term. Whatever works for you in this moment.

I am guessing that if you picked up this book, you may also feel something changing within yourself, a pull to something that you may or may not yet understand, and you are curious yet unsure about jumping into this unfamiliar world. The pull may be a feeling that there could possibly be a better version of you...of your life...of the world.

And then, there are those times when you begin to become more aware of serendipitous moments or feelings in your gut of knowing something is right or not right that give you pause. Maybe you even occasionally go to a psychic *just for fun* and although you are fascinated by the experience, you analytically justify it away. Should we even mention your yoga instructor (if you "do" yoga)—so calm, soft-spoken, and connected. How could someone like you, like us, have the intuition to sense and connect with the Universe like other spiritual people?

Are these things I mentioned even related? How would a person embark on this journey of spiritual self-discovery, and where does it lead you? "Can't I have a moment of self-awareness without it being a spiritual awakening?" you ask. Trust me—I have been there. And, if I am really being honest, I still go there after five years on this journey. So many questions to be answered.

Writing a book began presenting itself to me in the fall of 2018 at every turn. What has evolved over time is the audience for whom I would be writing the book. Although the title came to me out of the gate, I initially thought it was a memoir. Actually, I thought it was the publication of the yearlong journal I was guided to write—think *Bridget Jones* meets *Harry Potter*. I am thrilled this adventure has evolved into using the journal as a reference tool to write a guide for people like me. People who overthink things, who justify things, who analyze things, who question things, and who just might need to let go of some control.

I am your guide who will attempt to help you find your way from the analytical side of the river to the spiritual side. To cross this river, we will use the thirteen stepping-stones. Sometimes you will find another stone better suited for you, and that is okay too. In fact, you will likely hop from one stone to another and back again. Lastly, because of the nature of who we are, we will have access to both sides of the river in our lives.

As I began writing this version of the book, an intuitively gifted woman used the following example as a way to explain the awakening analyticals we are: "You can have a spiritually based business and remember to pay your quarterly taxes." This explains our duality. *We* are our own unique fusion of spiritual seekers.

Purpose

The purpose of this book is to furnish you with a few basic tools or lessons that you may take forward on your journey toward your truest self. The goal of this book is not to tell you exactly what you need to do, for you will discover this yourself.

The stepping-stones are merely that. Things you can begin to do now, or when you are ready, to discover the best version of yourself as you begin to contribute to raising the universal consciousness. Honestly, when I began my journey, my goal was healing and building a stronger me. I did not consider a universal consciousness into the equation. I did not realize then that by healing and discovering the truest version of self, we positively impact the universal consciousness. Whatever your mindset is at this point, the fact you are curious about investigating yourself and the spiritual side of life is amazing. This simple act already positively impacts your energy and the energy of those around you.

I am still on my journey, and what I have repeatedly learned and continue to be taught is that we need to let go of our desire for control. By working on this new version of ourselves, being present in our moments, and in trusting the Universe as we release control, we begin to enter the flow that is unique to us individually. I advise you to read each chapter, enjoy a few tales of my journey, and take from it what makes sense for your path at this moment of your journey.

Vision

A mentor once told me that when we take our life thus far and we place it onto a timeline to reflect on our life's journey to this point, we begin to see those instances and moments in time where the Universe attempted to reach us. With our rational minds leading the way for many of us in the world, the synchronicities are often analytically justified away, and life moves on until we are eventually ready to open ourselves to believing in the magic offered to us by the Universe.

As we each step forward into the truest version of ourselves, we will begin to help raise the universal consciousness. Although there are and have been some impressive people doing incredible things for the greater good in the world, the overall raised consciousness truly depends on each and every one of us. A good first step for us individually is to allow ourselves to open to believing (Chapter 1) in all this "craziness" and to begin or continue our self-healing (Chapter 2). It does take some work on our part. We carry wounds, fears, judgments—not only from this lifetime but from past lives and through the DNA of our ancestral lineage. Regardless, this is where we must focus our energies, and for many of us, it takes time as there is no quick fix. However, if every person out there were to invest the time to heal themselves and be present in their moments with gratitude, the vibration of the world…of the Universe would change in extraordinary ways.

My Story

When I look at my life's timeline, I have had a few moments in my life that altered its trajectory. Having grown up and attended college on the East Coast, after graduation my employer sent me to work in the Northwest with three weeks' notice instead of the originally planned California. This change took me to vastly different places with different experiences, some of which I am just beginning to understand now. When I was not in Seattle, my job had me traveling the roads of Central Washington and Montana. This young Maine girl got to drive cross-country, visit Alaska and Hawaii, Mexico and Canada—and many other US states in between during my seven years out West. And then, things began to change. Although an analytical person by nature, my last year in Seattle began to open my eyes to other possibilities of existence beyond the conservative corporate realm as the Universe began to speak to me.

As a perpetually single woman rapidly approaching thirty and ready to leave corporate life and move either to the islands to bartend or to other parts of the world to be trained by a Yogi, life quickly suggested otherwise for that moment in my journey, and I was redirected once again. On a trip back to the East Coast, I met my now former husband, the Universe spoke, and I followed the flow. I moved to Boston with another company, got married, started flipping properties, and had a baby girl. Yoga, magic, and the flow were put on the back burner. That said, I have always been amazed by the events that led me back East. I felt like something else had control over my life in that moment, and I simply sat back and watched it unfold. In 2006, my little family moved to Maine where my ex-husband and I had both grown up, had a second child—a little boy—and "life" happened.

It was not until our separation in 2015 that the light began seeping through again—another turn in my trajectory. As my sister and I went through simultaneous divorces and maneuvered the rigors of that process, this magical world began to unfold for us both.

As I mentioned, this path of self-awakening was not one I sought out, nor did I even realize I was stepping onto a path of self-awakening. The path does not always begin with a starting gate or buying a ticket for the show. In fact, some of us may not realize there was a race in which to participate or a show to see. For me, it began with subtle changes, new experiences, and healing. It took some time before I realized I had stepped onto the path of self-awakening.

Now, after five years of magical adventures and a lot of healing, here I sit writing a book. Stepping-stones have been placed in front of me all along my journey to guide me. These stones were sometimes different than the stones placed for others I know. Your stones will be placed for you. Until then, I would like to share with you some knowledge that has been presented to me and experiences that have served me well. If we are of similar mindsets, then I am hopeful these will serve *you* well as you get started on your journey.

How the Book Is Organized

The Spiritual Awakening of an Analytical Mind is structured to give you nuggets, or stepping-stones, to help you during your journey. Sometimes the nuggets may be more tangible practices you can incorporate now, and other times they may simply be an introduction to a topic you can investigate as you see fit. Think of this book as an outline, and now you have the opportunity to write your own story around it by gaining new knowledge, having new experiences, and discovering those items you wish to incorporate into your life.

With that, approach this book in a way that feels right for you—read it straight through or jump around when something speaks to you. The chapters are not mutually exclusive or necessarily in the exact order for you. Each stepping-stone will provide you with an opening explanation of the chapter, three subchapters to guide you, exercises you may incorporate into your practice, and a smattering of stories when they seemed relevant to share.

My biggest desire when deciding to write this book was to help people coming from a similar place as me. I wanted you to have one book, written in an honest, matter-of-fact way, to act as a baseline of information for you as you begin your journey—coming from the perspective of our linear way of thinking.

Please know you are not alone in being a hesitant participant on this path at the onset. Many of our paths up to this point may not seem compatible with this new path. Even our personalities may not seem compatible. But this is the path toward which the world is moving—a raised universal consciousness. And this is how we find ourselves in this unfamiliar place ready to embark on a new phase of our lives. Please be assured this path is an extraordinary one to undertake and will be a life-changing experience in the most positive way.

My Hope for You

Before we begin along our thirteen stepping-stones, there are three items of guidance I wish to offer you regarding your journey.

The first item is that we may begin this journey of self-awakening solely for ourselves, and that is often enough. With that said, as you begin to open and heal, you may feel a pull toward helping the greater good, which can take many forms. For some, it may even lead to a career change or forming a business in time. You will learn what makes sense for you, and the pull will likely evolve over time. Above everything, be kind to yourself. Your journey is your journey.

The second item is that each of us progresses through our journey at a different pace for a variety of reasons. Do not judge yourself against the journey of others, or them against your journey. This sounds adolescent, but the journey is such a new and unknown path for some of us, and our nature is often to compare ourselves to others—we like benchmarks. Please try hard to refrain from this. Some of us are tortoises and others are hares—both are great and get to where they need to go. Your journey is your journey.

The last item is that each person will develop their own toolbox of skills, from intuitive abilities to various certifications to modes of art. Once again, please leave judgment at the door. I have seen people with a few of the same certifications in their toolbox still end up at a different place on their journey. Your path will unfold over time. In Native tribes, individuals found their own power, and that was the gift they developed and brought to their people. All together the tribe had balance. We should not all be the same, and each of our gifts is important to the greater good. Your journey is your journey.

My hope for you is that the stepping-stones will act as guideposts, of sorts, as you begin your journey of self-discovery and self-awakening. Please know this path is remarkable. By stepping a foot onto the path, you will be forever changed in exceptional ways. In the simplest terms, walking this path of awakening is about becoming the best version of ourselves and allowing the positive energy, derived from our love, kindness, compassion, and gratitude, to ripple out into our lives— to our families and friends, our communities, our states and countries, the world, and the Universe. The action of becoming the truest version of ourselves makes all the difference to the universal consciousness.

As you begin this journey into a world that may not feel completely natural to your personality, I hope this book will offer you the feeling of reassurance and love from a kindred spirit—*as you create your own, unique path on your journey toward your truest self.*

Chapter One

Believing

Believing can be a tough concept for us analyticals to wrap our heads around. Let us give it some structure and definition to help our cause. What is believing? It can be an uncomfortable term when used in its broadest sense. It feels like a monstrous leap from analytical mind to believing because we all have our preconceived notions of what believing is. The dictionary defines believing as "something which we accept as true or where we hold an opinion." An example: "I believe that ABC Company has the best burrito." Oh, but wait. That is a fine statement. A burrito is a tangible item, and that statement is an opinion of the best-ness of the tangible item. Let's try this—"I believe the hawk I saw today was a sign from the Universe." Hold up! The hawk was likely just a hawk in search of a rodent to eat as it crossed my path. There is a believ-ability line for most of us.

Okay, so if we are stepping into this world of self-discovery, self-awakening, or spiritual awakening, "believing in what" becomes the question. Are we ready to believe in magic? That is a big leap, right? Perhaps we begin with believing in ourselves. Do you believe in your true greatness? How about happiness? Do you believe in true happiness? Do you believe you can have an impact on the world? There are so many levels of believing before we even get into believing in a higher being, God, the Great Spirit, or the Great Mystery.

In the end, the path to believing is different for everyone and, in a world where "seeing" is believing, some of us need repeated signs that this unseen world truly exists. For many people, it takes a trigger to kick us in the bottom to make changes—to see the possibilities of the world, our life, and ourselves differently.

When I began my journey in early 2016, I was still in a bit of a shambles. I was not officially divorced yet and was struggling with more things than I feel like writing at this stage of the game. This was my trigger. My push into believing was through my sister and her friend. In this post-divorce self-discovery process for us both, my sister began her spiritual awakening first. She had a sidekick in her good friend—now my good friend as well. Both women had always had *something* going on and were now spiritually taste-testing to see what spoke to them. They slowly began including me, at times somewhat reluctantly on my part, on this journey. Had they not been in my world, my awakening journey might have taken far longer.

What I had not realized then, as well, is I had become disconnected over time—not just through the marriage and divorce, but through life. Many of us fall into the "expectations" routine—college, job, marriage, house, kids, parent. We try to teach our children the importance of things we do not do for ourselves. Worse yet, we forget what is important, our priorities change, we analyze and judge to justify, we create less, maybe we lose a bit of our voice or ourselves, we compromise our truth, we stop believing or forget how to believe. Maybe we forget there is still magic out there in which to believe.

This was me. This is still many of us.

Even now, five years into this magical new world, I still find I am somewhat of a closeted spiritual junkie, for a lack of a better description. I still worry about the judgment of those who are not on this journey yet—of being perceived as "crazy" by the mainstream analytical world. My largest leap of faith was in May of 2020 when I officially kick-started my online presence and began writing this version of the book. It was my spiritual coming-out party and it felt great!

I placed Believing as the first chapter and stepping-stone of this book because I am guessing a few things have occurred in your life already that have piqued your interest in pursuing this self-awakening, maybe even call it a spiritual path. It is curious yet amazing, right? Try your best not to overanalyze the events in an attempt to justify them away. My advice to you is to begin to embrace your transformation.

As we progress into the chapter on Believing, we are going to discuss the strength of Opening the Door to Believing, Owning Our Journey, and Entering the Flow.

My hope for you in this chapter on Believing is that you take a deep breath and allow yourself to open to believing in more than the confines that many of us have placed on our existence. There is more in motion than simply our individual selves—even if we are unable to scientifically justify it all. Giving ourselves permission to sidestep our ingrained paths to discover more about ourselves and the Universe can be a little unnerving at times. I promise you, as a down-to-Earth Mainer from the conservative insurance industry, opening to believing is magic. And remember, believing can be as simple as believing in a better version of ourselves.

Opening the Door to Believing

We often begin this epic journey when we sense there is something bigger than the place where we are currently. Sometimes it takes a trigger, as I mentioned before, to give us the necessary shove onto the path, such as a death, divorce, job loss, feeling unsettled with our life, or even a pandemic.

I am going to share with you some of the early experiences that helped me to begin opening the door to believing. Remember, we are all different, and you will have your own experiences that help you believe. Those experiences will present themselves in your life when they are meant to arrive. For example, this book is in your hands because it is meant to be in your hands. It is not in everyone's hands. It is in your hands.

My story began with my doing exactly what I am telling you not to do…. analyzing and justifying; however, it cracked opened the door to believing. We may try to justify the door shut, but once the light can peek through, it is most likely open for good.

Believing Story 1—Yoga Nidra

As I mentioned, my journey began in January 2016. I was invited to attend a yoga nidra session with Reiki at a local yoga studio. I did not know what yoga nidra was—or even what Reiki was. My instructions from my dynamic duo were to "shut off your analytical brain." For those of you who do not know what yoga nidra is, I will explain in layman's terms or how I interpreted it at the time. Yoga nidra is a guided meditation where you lie comfortably in a yoga pose and you do not move or speak for forty-five minutes. I could not even fathom I would have the ability to handle the silence or, even less likely, refrain from speaking. Even the environment of such a class was outside my comfort zone. So much so that I felt like an impostor in the Zen-like atmosphere as we entered to take our spaces. Midway through the quiet session, the instructor came around and placed her hands on our bodies delivering Reiki. During her first pass through, I noticed her hands were on fire. It was later explained to me that the heat was from the energy of the other people in the class. *Accepted, but not understood.* As she put her hands on me during her second pass through, a white light blasted into my eyes, and my eyes began rapid movement back and forth. I was completely startled, yet I did not open my eyes to stop it. This little fact was pointed out to me later by my counselor who reminded me I could have opened my eyes had I wanted to do so. *True enough.* Nevertheless, I had to remain silently in position until the end of the session before I could ask questions. As I lay there waiting, I looked at the windows trying to justify to myself the possibility that a car across the street had shone its lights through the window, which would have explained the bright flash—although I then quickly deduced the angles were not right, and this was not a possibility. It was the wildest thing and may have been the shock I needed to crack open the door to believing in this magical world to which I was being introduced.

At the end of class, no one could really explain to me what had happened, because I asked as soon as the lights came back on, and they told me not to overthink it. It was eventually suggested that the blast of white light was stuck energy inside of me becoming unstuck. *This theory seemed like a feasible suggestion to me.* My counselor had a theory on the rapid eye movement piece (because I discussed it in our next session, still trying to find a justification) in that it was the polar sides of my brain trying to make sense of the experience—analytical versus spiritual. She compared it to EMDR (eye movement desensitization and reprocessing) used by therapists. *I liked this theory as a logical "scientific" explanation as well.*

And the door was cracked open. I was not looking for a spiritual awakening or even a self-awakening—perhaps a bit of self-preservation. Honestly, I was still in survival mode. The key was that I opened myself to these new experiences, I opened to believing in new possibilities…in a somewhat guarded sort of way.

Believing Story 2—Psychic

It was a one-two punch. Following the yoga nidra experience in January, in February I was asked if I wanted to go to a fair at the local gift and holistic shop, and then go to lunch. It sounded like a fun afternoon with the ladies, and they were always good for a few laughs, which I welcomed at this point of my life's journey. I met my sister at a park 'n' ride to carpool to the shop, at which point she informed me, once she had me in her car, that they had scheduled all of us with a psychic. After a small panic attack on my part, having never been to a psychic, my sister assured me it would be okay. Because the shop was busy, she and I would simply split a time slot. That meant we both would only have fifteen minutes, which meant I needed only one question—maybe two. After a few minutes, I determined that my question would be, "Will my kids be okay through this divorce?" I was ready. When we arrived at the shop, we suddenly learned we each had the full half hour instead. With not enough time to completely panic again, I resolved that I would survive, and my curiosity was getting the best of me by this time anyway. As I sat down with the psychic, I decided to play it cool…not to give her any information…see what she would come up with on her own (an original approach that I am sure they love). A half hour later, I had been shocked by things she knew; I had laughed…and cried. She was great, and I ended up visiting her again two or three times over the next six months.

In reflection, I determined in times when we are going through major life events, we occasionally need validation that everything is going to be okay. If a psychic satisfied the validation need for me, I was okay with it. This experience moved the believing pendulum a bit further.

One of my favorite stories from the psychic experience was seeing an incredible number of cardinals during spring and summer. There were so many cardinals around me in 2016, I thought there must be a bumper crop that year. I mentioned this to the psychic during one of my trips to see her over the summer. She said to me, "Oh, honey. There are not a lot of cardinals. They are a sign for you." To the books and computer I went! I researched a bit and discovered they were likely my ancestors coming to support me. They were everywhere! Darting in front of me in my car all the time. Unusually perched outside windows. On my lawn and in the trees around my house. It was crazy! This kept going until the divorce was finally final in August 2016, and then there was a break. This was my first experience that the Universe presents us with signs. If we watch and remain open, they are there for us. These days there are often cardinals around the house, again—I now just assume they are my ancestors and I have conversations with them, or I make their calls back to them. Crazy? Maybe a little.

Believing Story 3—Shaman

Fast-forward a year to the spring of 2017. My spiritual duo had begun seeing a shaman as part of their journeys, and together they decided to hold their first full moon ceremony in April as a step in their development of helping to spiritually guide others. They decided they would like me to attend; however, they felt I needed to go see the shaman prior to the ceremony. I threw out some reactive objections and then acquiesced without too much fight. Once again, my curiosity was piqued. I was excited yet had no idea what to expect. Who goes to see a shaman? What is a shaman? Who knew we even had shamans in Maine?

On April 7, 2017, I had my first ceremony with the shaman. He knew some of my life's deepest and darkest secrets, although that has not been the purpose of our sessions since. His energy was crazy. He was uplifting and positive, yet he gave tough love. He recognized new pain, old pain, family pain. He guided me to heal so I could further heal myself. At this point in my journey, I was still struggling with open wounds and seeing a counselor on a weekly basis. Sessions with the shaman became a second form of counseling for me. They also became an awakening. Many of these next chapters are life priorities brought into focus by my sessions with the shaman and solidified through additional experiences, meditations, and books. As I explained to my kids in those early days, it is not black magic—the shaman helped me focus on being a better person for myself, a better mother for them, a better steward for Earth, to be creative, and to work toward my truest self. Sessions with the shaman were a big part of my opening to believing—not only in the Universe but in the power of myself.

Again, your door openers may be quite different than mine. Simply be open to experiencing these new things that may be presented to you. That said, do not be pressured into an experience that does not feel right to you. You will know. You will feel it in your gut. Also remember we are each on a different path. Do not feel pressured by people who think their path is the only path and then impose judgment on those who do not follow suit. They may know what is best for *their* path, but *your* path is unique to you. I go back to one of my core beliefs in life. We can take nuggets from each of our experiences—the people we meet, the books we read, or the podcasts to which we listen—and create the right blend for us while letting the rest slip away. Try your best not to follow anyone blindly. The goal is for you to step into the version of your truest self—not a version of someone else.

Own Our Journey

One of my biggest struggles in jumping aboard the spiritual train was my own self-confidence and judgment—be it self-judgment, the fear of judgment of others, and, I guess, my own judgment toward this new world I was entering. As I sit here, five years into my journey, writing a book about spiritual awakening, I am still working on this one.

Personally, my core is practical. I have always worn a lot of black, gray, and tan. Life is linear, and there is an order to it. I like lists and spreadsheets. I was raised in the conservative insurance industry beginning at age eighteen. I have always cared what others think—too much. Sound familiar? Now let us take that personality and place it within the world of high-vibration people who are on their own spiritual journey. Gut instinct—justify it scientifically. Judge it. Consider the people a little crazy. Use humor to discount its validity. Or better yet, closet your involvement with it! I chose "all of the above."

Since this is still my biggest nemesis, or close to it, we can tackle this part of the journey together.

First, I want to begin with a quote by Albert Einstein that lends credibility to this dichotomy we feel, since we all likely perceive Einstein as an analytical mind, and therefore, objective and acceptable.

"The intuitive mind is a sacred gift and the rational mind is a faithful servant. We have created a society that honors the servant and has forgotten the gift."—Albert Einstein

Here is one of the great scientific minds telling us it is the intuitive mind that should be honored above the rational mind.

My wish for all of us is to own our self-awakening or spiritual transformation. Everyone knows us as practical; therefore, as we expose our newfound involvement in this nontraditional world, there could be raised eyebrows. What I finally asked myself in 2020 was, "What do I fear will happen if people know?" Judgment? Being ostracized in some way? Honestly, the majority of people are too wrapped up in their own stuff to worry about us, for the most part. Could there be a raised eyebrow or two? Sure. Does it matter? Not really! As we transition into our truest selves, don't we want the people who surround us to be those who love and support us on our journey, regardless?

This leads me to spiritual self-confidence. I found I would act as if I were merely *guilty by association* of hanging out with the magical people in my life as opposed to owning my actual involvement. We need to learn to own our involvement. The world would be a much better place if everyone operated at a higher vibration, a raised consciousness;

however, the mainstream population is not quite there yet. *We* need to be the people who step into the light and serve as a voice of reassurance for the other mainstreamers. As the rational mind representatives, we can explain the gift of the intuitive mind and be a bridge between the two—from one side of the river to the other.

As 2020 rolled around, I found a useful exercise to help push myself outside of the spiritual cocoon I had built, and maybe this will be helpful for you as well. I had written a list of ten intentions I wished to manifest during a new moon ceremony to begin the new year—and the new decade. We will go into more details regarding ceremony later. During each new moon of 2020, I updated the list by pushing myself a little further in certain areas. One intention was about stepping into my truth by telling X, Y, and Z people about this phase of my journey. I had one month before the next new moon to move forward with this intention. The act of telling people about my plan to go live with this "new me" was liberating. It felt like a weight had been lifted. This thing that had caused me stress was accepted by those around me and life moved on.

Please try to not let aspects of your transformation weigh you down. Be free! This whole awakening is quite magical. My advice to you is to own your journey the best you can—without imposing judgment on yourself. Remember, we are our own unique fusion of spiritual seekers and can pave the way for our fellow linear thinkers.

Entering the Flow

The title of this chapter is Believing. We have talked about Opening the Door to Believing and about Owning Our Journey. Now I am going to ask you to believe in a magical fairyland. I know—maybe too much, too soon.

Indulge me for a minute. Imagine a world where things come easily with little effort. Happiness fills our day. Love surrounds us. Money arrives when needed. The path unfolds before us. We feel peace and calm. Sounds amazing, right?

This is entering the flow. This is the end goal.

How do we get there? We step toward our purpose of aiding in raising the universal consciousness, and we relinquish control to the Universe as the two paths converge into the most awesome place.

Hold tight, my analyticals—I know the relinquishing control part is scary, and how do we aid in raising the universal consciousness? Well, we work through the other stepping-stones in this book in the order that makes sense for us individually. Honestly, we will jump back and forth during our journey, revisiting some of the stones multiple times because we will be in a different place with them. As I have mentioned, you will likely add your own stones as well. And, over time, with lots of work and healing, we will find this peace as we become part of the raised universal consciousness.

Recall the 2020 pandemic. Initially, we were asked to stay home for a couple of weeks to "flatten the curve" at the medical facilities, and then the "stay at home" was extended and extended again. Before we knew it, we had been at home for two and a half months (prior to the phase-in schedules). Maybe a twisted analogy; however, this is how things will unfold. In baby steps. All of a sudden, one day you will look at where you are and how far you have come, and you will smile—unlike with the pandemic.

Here is a simple example from my journey. As this magical world began unfolding in the early days, my kids and I would buy crystals and stones at a local shop. Mostly, they sat on our windowsills or dressers—and occasionally we would carry them in our pockets. I did not know much about them aside from the accompanying little piece of paper describing their qualities and attributes. Then one day, I felt the need to begin using a pendulum to determine which crystals or stones I should carry for each particular day. Soon thereafter, I *felt* the draw to create a crystal grid—with no knowledge of grid making. Every week or so I would feel the need to restructure the grid...and then I began meditations in front of it. At about the same time, I was guided to place certain crystals on my chakras to clear my energy centers. None of this was known, researched, or forced. It was intuition. Intuition that I did not think I had. Do you see what I am saying? The door cracked open a little, and then before I knew what had happened, I was being intuitively guided. In the beginning, I knew nothing about stones, crystals, grids, chakras, meditation, or clearing my energy centers. I did graze through a chakra 101 book; otherwise, things arrived when they were meant to arrive. Remain open and attempt to relinquish control to the Universe, and the magic seeps into your life.

That last sentence of relinquishing control to the Universe is really the key to the magical fairyland. Once we place our trust in the Universe, life simply becomes easier, happier, and more beautiful. That said, we all have some work to do to get ourselves to that point. Just remember that one day we will look at where we are and smile at how far we have come—and there will be unicorns and rainbows! I guess we each have our own interpretation of what happiness will look like for us.

This reminds me of one of the all-time great movies, *Avatar*. The main character, Jake Sully, gets left overnight in Pandora as a new, naive arrival to the planet. He creates a stick of fire so he can "see" in the dark. As he is quickly introduced to the wonders of Pandora, all the colors of the planet awaken, and he pauses in sudden awareness. Now, this was early in the movie and he still had a lot to learn, but his journey was beginning. What he lacked was fear, and what he eventually gained was awareness and gratitude for the planet and all living things. He learned how connected everything is from the trees to the animals to the people to the ancestors. The Natives of Pandora, the Na'vi, greet one another with, "I see you." Seeing others beyond their physical selves. When we believe, our awareness opens, and this magical world begins to appear before us.

Exercises

1) Friends who are already acquainted with this magical world will pull you into experiences you may not otherwise find on your own. It really does not matter initially what it is (psychic, tarot, Reiki, yoga nidra), for you will be deciding what modalities work for you over time; however, for this exercise, we are looking for someone to hold our hand or drag us outside our comfort zone a bit. Find your person and have an experience.

2) The less threatening ways to explore are to watch, listen, and read. You can do this in the comfort of your home with no one to judge your newfound curiosities. Find videos, movies, podcasts, articles, and books. Whatever catches your interest is right! They were placed in your path for a reason. I always look for one or two takeaways from each new experience.

3) If you are comfortable, find a holistic shop and go check out their inventory of crystals, stones, and such. It does not mean you have to buy anything—just window shop and feel the energy. Find the shop that feels right for you, that makes you happy when you are there. You will know.

4) Evaluate your current circle of family and friends as to who will support you as you look to discover your truest self. Sometimes it is necessary to step away from those who do not. It does not necessarily mean that they will never be in your life, but you need to give yourself the space to grow without judgment.

Book Recommendation

One book I will recommend to you out of the gate, and it was recommended to me early on by the shaman, is *The Raven's Gift: A Scientist, a Shaman, and Their Remarkable Journey Through the Siberian Wilderness* by Jon Turk. This is a story about believing in magic. It is a nonfiction adventure book by Turk, a scientist, and it bridged the gap between the analytical and spiritual for me.

Believing is a journey in itself. In this chapter alone we went from Opening the Door to Believing to the end result of Entering the Flow. The path between these two points can be a quick line from point A to point B or it can be like my typical approach to things—weaving our way through every nook and cranny between the two points. Our level of believing will evolve as we venture down our path and have the experiences from which we are meant to learn.

My advice for you going forward is to open yourself to new experiences that will expose you to new levels of believing in yourself, your life, the world, and the Universe. Feed yourself with the knowledge that speaks to you. Find the stepping-stones that make sense for your journey and remember you are creating a path that is unique to you as you step forward as your truest self. Own your journey as best you can. Begin to release control to the Universe. Initially, releasing control can be simply stating in a moment of stillness, "I surrender to Divine guidance all that is in my highest good." The meaning of the statement will grow in your heart as you further deepen your capacity to believe.

Chapter Two

Self-Healing

Even if you are not quite ready for the Believing chapter in its entirety just yet, this is a chapter you should begin now. Regardless of where your self-transformation takes you, healing yourself is an incredible gift to you, your children (whether born or unborn), your family, and your ancestors.

A Self-Healing chapter could be a book in itself and has been many times over. Little do many of us realize just how much healing we must do for ourselves. I know I did not realize. Of course, I believed I could either handle challenges myself, or I was fine and did not have anything in need of healing. And then there is the notion where the healing we must do is not simply for this lifetime! Believe it or not, my rational thinkers, we must heal our ancestral lineage and past lives too. I did not realize this either, nor could I have wrapped my mind around it. We will take this in small steps.

If we do a search of self-healing, many sites will pop up regarding self-healing through energy work. While energy work has wonderful benefits, I am more referring to the act of healing our inner self to allow ourselves the ability to step forward as our truest self with love, compassion, and gratitude—for ourselves and for others.

Much of self-healing is releasing what no longer serves us—and we will do this repeatedly on this journey. Some quick examples of things that no longer serve us are the bonds of former relationships, scars from childhood, self-doubt, fears of various things, and judgment toward self or others. Self-healing is about being kind to ourselves and to others. It is about gratitude—to ourselves, to others, to Mother Earth, to the spirits, to the animals, and the list goes on. Self-healing is about learning about ourselves and our lineage. Self-healing is a positive transformation of ourselves and how we approach life.

As we begin stepping forward, a simple way to be kind to ourselves is to develop a routine to begin our day with love, gratitude, and intention. As always, we will each find what works best for us individually, what we are comfortable including in a specific moment, and then (get ready) it will evolve over time.

From my experiences over the last five years, I have formed an ever-changing, and what seems ever-increasing, daily ritual. When I wake up in the morning, I attempt to begin with the following routine: take seven deep breaths to re-center myself; ask for protection from Brother Fire by placing rings of fire around myself and others (a practice from the shaman); recite the day's prayer by giving gratitude to all in my life, as well as a prayer to my guides; clear my chakras while in the shower (from Alberto Villoldo, PhD, *Shaman, Healer, Sage*); rinse with cold water for thirty seconds (morphed from Wim Hof); and end with a quick meditation to still my mind and set an intention to begin the day. In the snow-free months, I may go outside for much of this, along with placing my hands to the ground to transmute the energies no longer serving me while taking in the energies of Mother Earth. It may seem like a lot, but the whole ritual only adds about fifteen minutes to my morning.

Nothing I have mentioned above is crazy out there. Again, this is what works for me, and you will find your own morning ritual, but I do believe forming a daily ritual is a great practice in centering ourselves for this journey we are on. I remember reading about a person whose ritual is getting up super early, fixing himself a cup of tea, and creating a meditation around the mindful drinking of his cup of tea. This is his morning ritual before the household wakes up.

In this chapter, we are going to look at three categories of self-healing that I found useful on my journey: Outsourcing, Ceremony, and Genealogy. Once again, your journey will be unique to you; however, we all need a starting point, and so I will offer mine to get you started. And truly, many things discussed in this book can be classified under self-healing: nature, breathwork, creativity, journaling, music, dance, meditation, and the like. This road to awakening is all interwoven.

My hope for you in this chapter on Self-Healing is for you to hit the pause button on the routine of life. The pause will allow you to discover where you need work within yourself—and we all need work! For many of us, wounds we carry are glaring opportunities for self-healing. For others, we may need to get the pickaxe to dig out the wounds buried deep within our beings. Sometimes we can observe the behaviors of others to discover those same traits within ourselves in need of work. Our behavior may be to a lesser degree than what we have observed, but seeing those traits in another can make us aware of them within ourselves.

Working on and embracing our self-healing allows us to walk this new path with a brighter light than previously. It allows us to step forward into the raised universal consciousness and to contribute toward it. If you have ever gone two...three...four days without a shower, think how great it feels once you finally shower to remove all the accumulated grime from your body. Self-healing is a bit of showering our inner being—perhaps after years...or lifetimes...or generations of neglect. Embrace your self-healing. It becomes a lighter existence without carrying the baggage!

Outsourcing

Self-healing is about healing ourselves. Said another way, we are ultimately the person accountable for healing ourselves. No one can do it for us; however, there are tools available for us to trek the path of self-healing with a little help from a friend, a professional, a mentor, and such—and those are all good too. I found outsourcing a fun word to use as a subchapter here. Subcontracting could have been a fitting word as well. By using these words, I am hopeful they will help make the point that we can bring in "the experts" to assist us in accomplishing this project of ours, but ultimately, we are responsible for the finished work—the end result. We are the general manager or the general contractor of our own self-healing. *I love that you understand what I am saying here!*

I am going to offer you examples of subcontractors I used and am using on my path. The examples I chose and will discuss cover mind, body, and spirit. Keep in mind, none of these things need to be far-fetched. Many of us may even be incorporating some of them into our life now. We keep stepping forward as we heal, digging a little deeper with each step. Like Shrek said in the original *Shrek* movie, "Ogres are like onions. Onions have layers. Ogres have layers." Keep peeling away those layers. Heal ourselves.

Mind: Let us begin with counseling as the first example. Many of us begin our self-healing on the couch of a counselor even before we realize we are embarking on a journey of self-awakening or self-discovery. We may be able to place this self-healing modality on the analytical side of self-healing. It is not crazy unusual. It is a rather mainstream accepted practice nowadays. It is even covered by our group health insurance policies!

In my younger adult years, my circle did not speak of counselors, nor did we go. As sales representatives for an insurance company, we knew this little snafu would show up on a person's medical history and make it more difficult to obtain certain insurance policies. Back then, it was better to swallow any unsettled feelings than to seek help in resolving them. Shedding the stigma ingrained in my way of thinking was an early step for me in the process of self-healing, but it did not occur until almost forty. And then, aside from a two-year hiatus in the middle, I visited my counselor faithfully for the next seven years.

Depending on our individual situation, there can be so much to unpack about our lives. For me, my counseling sessions gave me a place where I could speak to an unbiased listener. There were no repercussions from what I said in that space, and she could respond without an agenda. There were no lingering feelings from one family member toward another, as there would have been had I shared within my circle instead. It was a safe space even if it was solely for me to say things out loud at times and then process the thoughts or feelings myself.

As I ventured down the road of self-healing, I came to a point where I realized I was going into these sessions to replay things that no longer mattered. I had gained the tools to better process life events, and I was in a different place in life. I was ready to heal and move on. Now three years removed from my counseling sessions, I do think I could benefit from an occasional session as layers are removed and new discoveries are made or as I maneuver through my own unchartered waters of parenthood. There is something safe about having a place to verbally work through thoughts and feelings outside of our inner circles.

Only you know if you would benefit from counseling, but please do not hold judgment toward yourself if you do decide to seek it out. Life can be a lot at times. As you search for the tools to healthily process situations, it is a place to unload some baggage. The other thing to note is that more and more counselors are now combining Eastern and Western philosophy into their practice for a more integrated holistic healing covering mind, body, and spirit. Do your research and find the right fit for you should you decide to pursue this avenue.

Body: Taking care of our bodies is a wonderful tool to incorporate into our self-healing. I have a friend who gets after me every now and then on the importance of bodywork. She advises me to schedule monthly services to take care of myself. By bodywork, I am referring to all forms of massage, in addition to craniosacral therapy, myofascial release, acupressure, and reflexology—to name a few. For myself, I think energy work, facials, manicures, and pedicures are forms of taking care of our bodies as well. Very few of us are good about scheduling any of these treatments on a regular basis. We need to consider these services as a part of our self-healing routine as opposed to a treat or a guilty pleasure.

Many of these practitioners are very intuitive as well. With their hands on our bodies, they can sometimes read what is happening within us. As one intuitive practitioner friend told me during a facial, "You need to schedule a massage with Sally; you have anger in your ass!" I still laugh at this. When I went to see Sally to work out the "anger in my ass," she informed me she kept seeing yellow birds on my back, which she felt represented innocence. Interestingly, about the time she was seeing the yellow birds, her instrumental background music turned to a rather loud full version of "Return to Innocence" by Enigma. You cannot make up this stuff! Fascinating, even if we cannot explain it away, and a fun little bonus to the bodywork we are receiving.

We all know bodywork can help address those tight spots in our physical body, but there are emotional benefits as well. If you are able, try to incorporate bodywork into your self-healing routine.

Spirit: When the time feels right for you or the opportunity presents itself, a spiritual mentor is a gift. For me, my spiritual mentor came in way of time with a shaman a little over a year into my journey, as I mentioned previously. He was another form of counseling in the early days of our time, and always a teacher and guide. He has helped shift my mindset from victim to warrioress. He taught me the importance of raising up myself, which will then raise up my children. He taught me to honor nature and to have gratitude for all in life. He gave me lessons on the negative effects of projecting pity on ourselves and others rather than projecting in a positive light. He taught me to approach life's tougher moments with the mentality of *what am I meant to learn from this situation* instead of succumbing to instinctual reactionary behaviors. I was taught individuals come into our lives for a reason, and we should pause to see what it is we are to learn from them. I was taught to be kind to others, for we do not know what lesson they were meant to learn during this lifetime. I learned to release my anger for it does not serve me. There are many, many lessons. In totality, it is about walking in our light and finding our truest selves.

Now, I will step back. If you had told me a few years ago that I would spend time with a shaman, I would have laughed. I did not know anything about the practices of a shaman, and my ignorance would have filled in the blanks with judgment. Yet a shaman reminds us about what is important in life and guides us in the changes we need to make on this path of self-awakening. I am grateful to have been presented with this opportunity in my life, and although I no longer see him as often, I continue to learn from his lessons as I walk my path.

Begin to give yourself time—time for honest reflection to see what you need for your mind, allow yourself time for your body, and see what calls to spark your spirit. You will feel the pull to what is right for you in this moment of your journey. Maybe a yoga class will be where you find the connection that resonates through your mind, body, and spirit. Allow yourself to explore. Most of all, be patient with yourself. This journey takes time, and often there is much healing for us to do. Taking care of our bodies and giving our minds the space to process our lives is a beautiful gift to ourselves as we begin our journey.

Ceremony

No, I have not lost my mind. I am putting Ceremony as an early tool to aid with self-healing. Bear with me a moment.

Ceremony was not part of my vocabulary until a year into my transformational journey. When the practice of ceremony was introduced to me, I may have thought it a bit crazy, yet I took those awkward steps outside of my comfort zone. But when we think about it, ceremony has been an accepted part of our mainstream lives, even with those of us who were not raised with religion. At a bare minimum, we partake in weddings and funerals—ceremonies. For those raised in churches, temples, and other religious houses, there are many more ceremonies held and much more frequently. And then there is formality and reverence brought to these ceremonies, as well.

So, you ask, how is ceremony part of our self-healing?

What I have learned over the last few years is that ceremony shows the Universe we are showing up to do the work necessary to step forward toward our truest self. Being one of those individuals not raised in the church, it is taking the step of acknowledging there is something much bigger than our individual self at play. We can call it whatever we feel most comfortable in calling it. Some may be okay with God. I lean toward Great Spirit. For me, this was a *huge* step. The more we release control and open to accepting and believing, the more this presence shows up in our life.

Aside from a cord-cutting ceremony performed by the psychic, my introduction to ceremony was a Native American ceremony where

I learned about the use of copal, resin from certain trees—pitch to us laymen. We mostly use copal from local cedar trees here in Maine. Again, not too far out there considering incense has been used in religious ceremonies predating Christianity. This ceremony first taught me the process of Native ceremony, the gratitude and honor to be displayed, prayer, the reverence to the directions and to Mother Earth, along with clearing our energy with copal before proceeding to ceremony. Prayer had never been part of my life, but within this ceremony with the natural world, it finally felt right.

In my humble opinion, the simplest and most consistent place for a person to begin holding ceremony is with the new moon and the full moon. Not only do these ceremonies begin a practice for us, but we begin aligning with the lunar cycle. We can look up the days and times where the new and full moon fall in our time zone each month, and we can look up the meaning of that particular event for that particular month, for example, a new moon in Pisces. We can look up ceremonial rituals to hold in the comfort of our own space as well. The site I used a lot early in my journey was www.foreverconscious.com. It is a tame site for us new to the game and offers a detailed description for us to follow—with bullet points or step-by-step directions, structure. Most often, we are setting intentions on the new moon (I will have more gratitude for the gifts in my life) and releasing what no longer serves us on the full moon (I release judgment of myself and others). Give the site a look. I think you will be pleasantly surprised by the simplicity it offers to those of us new to this journey. It is a great place to begin a practice.

I was fortunate my sister and friend began holding new and full moon ceremonies. Even though I felt a bit out of place, it brought me together with others on this path and helped me to get more and more comfortable with the ritual. I remember on my way to my first ceremony, I asked about this "list of intentions" that we were to write, and I verbally compared it to making a to-do list for the next month. Although I was quickly corrected, in actuality, it really is a bit of a to-do list—a spiritual to-do list, perhaps. Our list offers our intentions we are putting out into the Universe; however, they do not manifest without being tended to. For those of us who have grown up in business, we set our goals, and then we work toward them. Much the same with a little magic sprinkled in for good measure.

As a side note, ceremony becomes even more powerful when held with a group. When we bring together a group of people all operating at a higher vibration, magic will likely follow. By higher vibration, I mean people living life in a more positive place—with love, gratitude, happiness, and a truer sense of self. We are becoming higher-vibration people as we continue our journey of self-awakening. On the other end, lower-vibration people focus more on the toxic emotions and the less healthy aspects of life. We can find some great scientific articles on vibration if we feel the need to justify this concept. Even though we are opening to believing, sometimes a little science can help ground us, ironically.

How does ceremony enter into self-healing?

Ceremony brings reverence, formality, honor, recognition, reflection, and gratitude to self-healing. The time during ceremony feels like the pause button has been pushed on life to allow us the space to self-heal. In this moment of ceremony, we are setting intentions, releasing what no longer serves us, offering gratitude, asking for guidance, being still, sharing love, entering an honest place, and feeling hopeful. Ceremony can be very emotional. When sitting in these moments, we can often sense something greater than ourselves in motion.

Genealogy

This one was within my comfort zone—researching ancestors. I have a funny feeling this is where you will feel comfortable as well. How researching our ancestors ties into a chapter on Self-Healing makes sense to me now; however, it was a long and twisted road to get me to this point. For this subchapter, I am simply going to share with you my journey along this path as I think doing so will offer you the clearest insight into how genealogy can aid in self-healing.

After a few months of seeing the shaman, he brought up ancestors and nudged me toward researching my lineage. I am a very literal person and, occasionally, topics during my sessions with the shaman were not always clear to me. This was a new world, and I often nodded my head in understanding although not truly understanding things. But genealogy—I could sink my teeth into this, so I dove into researching.

I pulled out my genealogy research from a senior project way back in 1989. I had enjoyed doing the research back then, and now we have computers and sharing of information online! Using the former project as a starting point, I spent hours researching the different family lines off and on over the next few months. Part of the research was to determine if we had any Native blood in our family and part was purely to fill in our ancestral lines. This was much of my magic for a few months. I had no idea if this path would take me anywhere, but I kept going out of the sheer fascination of the history and learning their stories. And in my empathic nature, I tried my best to keep the research of each family line even—as not to make any of my deceased family members feel bad that I was giving one line more attention than another. You can laugh.

The process of digging into the family lines gave me a connection to the past. It prompted conversations with older family members to hear their stories, along with the stories they knew of those who had already passed, and which they were able to share. I found old family pictures online and received others from family members. Census from years ago filled in gaps and outlined the story of deaths from war or disease. Living in Maine, we have Henry David Thoreau's *The Maine Woods* to give us a recounting of the Maine landscape in 1846. His writing provided me with an accurate picture of Maine during the period that I was researching. It helped connect me to my ancestors.

Something that did not seem to have any relevance to my genealogical research began around this same time as well. While playing tennis, I turned my ankle and then turned it again while hiking over the summer. After months of the ankle not healing, and having pain in it all the time, I finally went to a sports therapist. The X-rays were fine, and there was nothing they could do to help. The pain would continue for a full fifteen months. Now…while I had been researching my ancestors, I discovered a census from 1880 that listed my great-great-grandmother as "adopted, a vest maker, disabled by a chronic sprained ankle." Here began my true connection to my ancestors, and it is as crazy as you may be thinking, by the way! A story for another day.

Along with my ancestral research, I continued my sessions with the shaman, continued new and full moon ceremonies, and began opening myself to believing. I took the next step of holding ceremonies at home by myself, and more things began to occur. I felt the urge (intuition) to have my genealogy grid next to me during ceremony. Back then, I had begun using a pendulum often—as I did not fully trust my intuition. I sensed my ancestors wanting to come through. I cannot explain it other than the thought passed through my awareness or I sensed it. I would use my pendulum to determine which line wanted to come through. In the beginning, I asked questions about a specific family line, and then "they" showed up. I could sense healing needed to be done. We all carry the DNA of our ancestors; therefore, we carry familial traits within us— good and bad. My sister and I began holding healing sessions for our ancestral lines. Both of us would "get the message" and would then call one another to schedule a time. Sometimes we were not fast enough, and a message of urgency would get to us as well. One by one we began clearing and healing our lines. We would sit in ceremony and heal wounds and traits of the past—from physical and emotional abuse to the pain of giving a child up for adoption. They each came to us loud and clear over a few months until they did not—at least not for this purpose or with such urgency.

For a person beginning this journey, I understand how crazy this sounds, but I promise it is true. I now feel this connection to my family that I previously did not have to this extent. I understand some of my traits and those of my parents and grandparents that now make sense. I am hopeful that in understanding our family, I can help prevent certain traits from carrying forward through my children while nurturing the many loving traits. I would highly recommend learning where you come from for many reasons, including self-healing. It is a really beautiful experience.

In my house sits a table from my fourth great-aunt gifted to me by my grandmother before she passed more than twenty years ago. On the table are pictures of most of my grandmothers going back to 1832. At least once a day, I acknowledge them and give gratitude to them. Every morning I give gratitude to all those in my life, either from the physical plane or spiritual realm, and my ancestors are always part of that. Whether we acknowledge our ancestors' presence with us or are unaware of it, they are here with each of us, nonetheless. Our ancestors paved the path for us and are available to guide us. Please do not be afraid to acknowledge them, give gratitude to them, and even ask them for their guidance or protection when you are ready.

The reason I have included Genealogy in this chapter on Self-Healing is that we come from a similar place, and I feel strongly about what this process has brought into my life. I am hopeful you will feel the same— to whatever degree your research takes you. Researching feels tangible. There is a substance to it. For me, it was a grounding tool in a way. The bonus is making the elders in our families incredibly happy to have someone researching the family tree and listening to their stories.

Exercises

1) Breathing is a great exercise regardless of where you are in your journey. We often forget to truly breathe. I have found a good way to stop the race is to take in a slow deep breath and fill your lungs halfway, hold the breath for four counts, and release slowly. Do this for seven breaths. It can help stop the mind chatter, re-center your being, and in the wee hours, it puts me right back to sleep.

2) Make a list of tough experiences you have encountered in your life. To the right of each item, write what you learned from the experience. Find the light. As you walk forward, try to approach new situations with this thinking in real time instead of being reactionary. This approach can take away some of the emotions when you think, "This is an experience on my journey. What is it here to teach me?"

3) Pull up the upcoming new and full moon schedules for your location. Use www.foreverconsious.com or another website that resonates with

you and begin attuning to the lunar cycle through new and full moon rituals. You may be able to intuitively create your own ritual or ceremony when you feel ready.

4) Begin exploring your family and ancestors. Create a genealogy chart—it does not have to be anything fancy—and complete what you already know first. This is your starting point to connect you to what is available online, in town halls, and in graveyards. And most importantly, talk to your living family. Ask them about those who have passed and about family stories. They love being asked and sharing what they know. Sometimes the simple act of connecting with your family in these discussions is healing for everyone involved.

Self-healing is truly a gift, albeit one of those gifts that comes with a bit of work, like receiving a pet as a birthday present. As we ventured through the chapter, we discussed Outsourcing to subcontractors to aid us with our healing of mind, body, and spirit; the healing rituals of Ceremony; and the beautiful benefits of learning about our ancestors through our Genealogy. As mentioned at the start of the chapter, there are many more modes of self-healing for us to explore. We need only begin, and then step forward as we continue to peel back the layers.

My advice for you going forward is to approach each step of self-healing as an exciting opportunity to deliver you to a better place. Remember to be kind to yourself and others as you work on your healing. Leave judgment, from past or present, at the door. Creating a daily ritual will help ground you as you clear the clutter. Finally, being fully present with each of these moments, with every moment, creates a beautiful path for you as you focus on creating the best version of yourself.

Chapter Three

Solitude

Solitude can have a bit of a negative connotation when we hear the word. In fact, I struggled with whether to use it as a chapter title. Defined, solitude means, "the quality or state of being alone" according to our friends at Merriam-Webster. It is the appropriate word for this chapter. So why should being alone have a negative connotation in my mind? I like my time alone. Although I am alone, I am not lonely. Actually, the more layers I pull back within myself, the less lonely I am when I am alone. Yet, as a society, we feel the need to fill our time-space, to reduce solitude. Many parents do this with their children's time—to keep them busy and off electronics. (Which we should mention, being alone with our electronics does not count as healthy solitude.)

The question is, "How will solitude help us in our self-awakening?" I do not anticipate this explanation will be as much of a leap as convincing us to believe. Likely, we will embrace a little solitude, a little going within. Regardless of where we fall on the analytical spectrum, introvert to extrovert, sitting with oneself in thought or reflection can be healing, self-realizing, and productive for us. We can embrace solitude in a variety of ways by creating space for ourselves—both in time and place. If we fall closer to the extrovert end of the spectrum, creating a moment of stillness may be a little more challenging. I know it was for me. I thought my brain would explode at times—a few ants in my pants as well. Start small and do not judge yourself. It is not a competition.

Allowing ourselves to realize that solitude is not "nonproductive" time is a concept with which many of us likely struggle. The generation in which many of us grew up has an expectation of productivity—you work hard, you keep busy, you fill your time. As a result, we may have a pang of guilt associated with stopping for solitude—even if it is self-imposed guilt ingrained in our being. So we may need to begin small. Allow those moments for ourselves even if it is a quick five or ten minutes in meditation or sitting alone outside finding our peace.

Throughout my journey, some of my most profound healing, thoughts, creative ideas, and self-development have come through this amazing space. The space we provide ourselves with solitude is where the real magic can occur. Many of us are coming from a place full of mind chatter and angst. The thought of sitting down and clearing the chatter can often lead to more angst as we think about all the things we could be…should be doing. But it is time to stop. Allow ourselves the gift to stop. Begin with small moments of time.

Through this chapter of Solitude, we will talk about Journaling, Self-Reflection, and Meditation. You will discover on your journey that all three are intertwined. You may meditate, which spurs the need to reflect on the meditation before you journal about it.

My hope for you in this chapter is that you develop a routine of solitude suitable for you. As always, know your routine will grow, change, and develop as you do. My other hope for you is that you approach this chapter with a sense of opportunity at all you can discover about yourself, both in this space of solitude and on this journey as a whole. We are complex creatures with a lot held within our bodies and minds. Providing yourself the space to investigate all who you are, as well as allowing yourself to dream of the new you who lies ahead, is such a gift. A gift you deserve.

Self-Reflection

It is time to stop. Turn off the mind chatter button for a bit, and for some of us, the mouth button as well. I feel completely comfortable in telling you that you will not run out of topics as you sit in self-reflection. We can go back to Shrek's onion layers. We each have many layers within ourselves to examine. Self-reflection is so versatile as well—much like a wine. You can use it alone or pair it with a nice journal or meditation. You can use it in nature, in a cozy place you have created, or in front of an altar. It all sounds quite lovely really.

We will go back to Merriam-Webster for a definition of self-reflection: "self-examination." That was quick and simple! I guess it makes sense, but what does it truly mean? It means we need to dissect who we are and establish who we want to be. If there are gaps between the two, how do we move from point A to point B? We can look at this from the eagle's perch, a high-level examination, to a mouse's viewpoint of the smaller inner workings of our being. Do you see just how many moments of self-reflection there truly are? Who we are as a person in general, how we treat others, what we want to achieve in life, how we parent, our health, our happiness, what is important to us, our relationship with another—and we can go on and on. Please do not stress out. It is not a race. The fact we are embarking on this path is tremendous. Take it one step at a time. My feeling is the first step is simply the awareness we have room to grow and recreate our world.

I used an example of two perspectives in the above paragraph, an eagle and a mouse. This may sound a little "out there" at this point in our journey, but we can learn a lot from the creatures of our planet. Yes, it is true. Every animal has qualities they embody. At certain times of our day, our year, our life, embodying the qualities of certain animals can provide us with guidance. Now, please hold that thought for a moment.

Have you heard of oracle cards? I had not. If we go to any metaphysical store, we can find them, or we can purchase them online. They are a fun tool as we begin our journey. I bought a couple sets of cards during the first year of my journey. The theory is that we will intuitively pull a card from the deck that makes sense for us in a moment of our journey. The decks typically come with a book to explain each of the cards. One of my first sets of cards was Native Spirit by Denise Linn. What I love about this deck is it not only gives us the meaning of the card, but also what "Native Spirit wants us to know," and then offers us a journey if we would like. It does not mean we do everything it suggests every time, but it brings our awareness to a topic on that day. It could be as simple as "you need to purify—drink more water." There are many oracle decks available, depending on what speaks to you.

Another popular deck is Medicine Cards by Jamie Sams and David Carson. This deck is based on the creatures of our planet and offers much insight into their qualities—as with eagle and mouse from above. The intent is not to sit and read the book, but to intuitively pull a card from the deck, and then read the piece for the animal on that card. After we read the wisdom, we can reflect on how those qualities pertain to us and our life. Self-reflection.

Yes, I know. This is stepping outside of what may make logical sense to many of us. I completely understand. I do. This is a small step, though. Some of us may not be completely ready to embrace the full enchilada of this journey just yet, but it develops. Remember my creed: take from people and things the nuggets that make sense for you at this moment in your journey, and let the rest slip away. For me, early on especially, stepping on and down this awakening path seemed overwhelming at times—there is a lot to do and absorb. Taking five minutes to pull cards made me feel like I was participating in whatever was happening on my new path, and then the card itself brought my mind to an awareness— maybe just for a moment or maybe for the entire day. The awareness could be as simple as having gratitude for what we have been given in life. We can take from it whatever it is we are ready to take from it at that moment. A little self-reflection. Also, how frequently we pull cards will vary over time. There is no right or wrong.

Self-reflection is a great assistant as we journal and meditate as well. As we are quickly learning, many stepping-stones and tools are intertwined, and self-reflection is no exception. As we move forward on our path with all these new tools, we are taking the steps toward the best version of ourselves. Find your moments of self-reflection and moments to process your inner self as you move from point A to point B.

Journaling

If you are anything like me, you have attempted this journaling "thing" a few times in your life to no avail. Multiple times in my life I have decided to begin a journal, thought I needed to get the journal up to speed, wrote until my hand wore out, and then did not journal again. Then, there is the other end of the spectrum where my grandmother journaled every day, year after year. It was a journal of facts—the weather, what the farm sold that day, who stopped by the house.

What I am learning about journaling is that consistency is the key. Like anything, if we do it consistently enough, it becomes a habit, a routine part of our day. The other piece I have finally figured out is we do not have to write a lot unless we have a lot to say on a given day. The key is consistency not how much we write. The great thing about journaling is there is no wrong way! This is our sacred space. State the facts of the day like my grandmother, use the journal to work through our feelings or keep track of our nightly dreams. We have all heard people tell us or others that if we have strong feelings about someone or something, write it down like we are going to mail the person a letter. Often the very act of writing it down soothes the situation, and no letter needs to be sent. Use your journal in this way to work through some areas in need of self-healing if that makes sense for you.

Another nice journal starter is to use writing prompts to begin our self-reflection. Find a prompt or a topic that we would like to explore, and simply begin writing until we feel ready to stop; or set a timer for ourselves to see what we write in, say, ten minutes. This is a great way to process our thoughts, feelings, and even buried emotions. There are so many ways for us to begin.

Do we write longhand or create an online journal? I love handwriting things and love a nice "to-go" book; however, when I was guided to begin documenting my journey, I went online. At the time, I was about two and a half years into my journey, my intuition began opening, and I began daily meditations and journeys. Every day was a crazy adventure that I did not fully believe. And so every day I wrote. I would meditate or journey, reflect on what had occurred, research much of it because the gaps in my knowledge were significant, and finally, I would write. For this particular journal, I attempted to keep the writing purely about the spiritual path I was embarking on. I am thankful to have the journal from that period, as it documented an important phase of my journey. As that phase ended, I continued a daily journal and found I began moving to a more day-to-day log, which was okay too. It kept me in a routine. When I went virtual with my adventure in 2020, my daily journaling waned over the summer months. My writing shifted to writing the stories of inspiring women, building an online presence, and writing this book. These writing excerpts became my journal, of sorts. I am certain that someday soon I will return to my daily journaling.

Your journal will develop as you see fit and will change over time. Stay fluid with your expectations of yourself. Since this is a chapter on Solitude and introspection as part of your self-awakening journey, I would recommend that you push yourself to use your journal for a little self-healing, a little self-reflection, and a little dreaming. Explore yourself.

Meditation

You know our world is changing when what is deemed acceptable to the mainstream population includes modalities and practices that work on our inner healing and raising the consciousness of ourselves and the Universe. Going back to the odd analogy I used earlier of the 2020 pandemic and how the two weeks of quarantine became two to three months of "stay-at-home" orders, a similar concept goes for what is considered generally accepted practices to the general population. Massage was massage until our therapists learned polarity and Reiki and began incorporating energy work into their practices. Yoga, Western yoga that is, was a form of exercise until it connected and opened practitioners to their minds, bodies, and spirits. Now connected, open, and seeking more—meditation became a new norm. And with a twist, mindfulness. Think how mainstream mindfulness, being in the present, has become for adults and children. People are aware of it. It has been brought into the schools. So yes, these have all become mainstream—Step One! The awareness has been established. These practices are now acceptable to the norm. Step Two is for the general population to actually begin these practices with a level of consistency.

For our discussion, let us focus on the art (and arguably the science) of meditation. According to Deepak Chopra, "*Meditation is the progressive quieting of our mind, until we reach the source of thought, which in wisdom traditions are the realm of our soul and spirit. In this domain of awareness there is infinite creativity, synchronicity, the power of intention, and freedom from limitations.*"

This sounds enchanting, though a bit overwhelming for many of us. For us rational thinkers, let us simply consider that meditation does for our brains what exercise does for our bodies. I think we can take that further because we know the scientific effects our minds can have on our physical bodies—and vice versa.

There are an endless number of sources on the internet providing their interpretations of the meaning of meditation and the benefits of meditating. I am not going to pretend to know more than those sources, and I recommend you investigate what works for you. I know my meditation experiences have simply unfolded and evolved as I was ready for the next step. My journey was never about following an exact script, and that works for me. Do your own research and form a practice that works for your being.

I will provide you with one source who gave me guidance and I was pleasantly surprised and grateful to receive it when it arrived. As one does, I found my way to watching *The Enlightenment* (2017), directed by Natalie Fuchs, which follows the journey of a few individuals during the Buddhist Kalachakra Initiation with His Holiness the Dalai Lama. He is a very funny man who takes the opportunity during this initiation to review some basic Buddhist teachings to the mass crowd—likely to their surprise. Although the book you are reading is not about any particular belief system, I found the Dalai Lama's step-by-step teaching of the physical aspect of meditation helpful to my meditation practice. You can find his guidance from 0:37:25 to 0:39:37 in the film.

By developing physical calm for our body through a proper meditation posture, a mental calm is created allowing for more clarity to be brought to our meditation practice.

Although I cannot do his word-for-word description full justice, I will summarize his instructions here. We should situate our cushion or folded blanket so that it is raised about two and a half to three inches in the back and less in front as we sit into lotus position while maintaining a straight torso. Our hand placement has our left hand under our right hand with our two thumbs coming together at our navel. While ensuring our straight spine, we should attempt to relax our shoulders. As for our head, it should be slightly tilted forward, along with our chin slightly lowered, and lips and teeth slightly apart with our tongue against our palate—all while attempting to focus our attention on the tip of our nose. In our proper position, we can now breathe. Our breath should be calm—not too noisy, not too slow, and not too fast. Just calm. (Interpretation from His Holiness the Dalai Lama, *The Enlightenment* (2017).)

Now that we know how to physically meditate properly, let us bring in the reality of meditation for many of us. Early meditation for me was purely stilling my body—forget my mind. I could sit there for five minutes at best while I thought about all the things I needed to be doing or wondered how in the world a person clears one's mind for meditation, and then I was done. I did not "get it"—nor did I research it. I accepted meditation was "not my thing." Sound familiar?

So how did this change to a place where I can now peacefully sit in meditation for as long as seems appropriate? Baby steps, once again! Your journey will be yours, but this is how things evolved for me. First, without an awareness of my intent, I began an overall calming of my space. As a self-professed sports radio junkie for two decades who spent my entire work life in my car, I shut off my car radio one day early in my journey and I have never turned it back on—aside from teenage music when my kids are with me. For those who know of Boston sports radio particularly, it is a negative mess of discussions. Leaving it behind calmed my space—calmed my mind and carried over outside the car. Then one day, I turned on sound frequencies for your chakras (I know, right?) while I was working out....and then while cleaning the house.

By the time I sat down for a true meditation after a few weeks of that, I was guided to pull up this beautiful Tibetan meditation music, and my meditation world changed forever. I realized I am attuned to audio. It can be as simple as singing bowls playing, and I can settle into meditation quickly. I had no idea! For you, it could be simple audio like me, it could be guided meditations, or it could be other triggers, like focused breathing. Play with different sensory props that may work for deepening your meditation practice. You will discover what works for you in quieting the mind chatter. Once I got to this point, I learned the proper posture from the Dalai Lama, and my meditation practice was complete—at least for now, I think.

From my own experiences and from readings, I would recommend two things as you develop and incorporate meditation into your life. Find a space and time for your daily meditation, and then do your best at creating a routine for your meditation practice. There could be times when the space or time is not available, and that is okay. The pandemic threw my meditation ritual for a loop. I now do my best to fit it in at some point in the day, and eventually I will get back to my "normal" schedule. In the Self-Healing Chapter, I discussed creating morning rituals to center ourselves to begin our day. I mentioned the man who begins every day using the mindful act of drinking his cup of tea for his morning meditation before the household awakens. This practice is perfect for him. Find what works for you.

We will find other times and other places to complement our meditation practice as we go along—especially in nature: in the woods, on a mountain, by the ocean, or in the middle of a lake. We will all discover our sacred spaces. Nature's sounds and sights make beautiful aids to meditation.

Exercises

1) The next time you go to the metaphysical shop, which you have already discovered, check out the oracle card section. Play around with the cards and see what speaks to you. You can usually purchase a deck

for fifteen to thirty dollars. Use whatever deck you purchase as a prompt for self-reflection and self-awareness.

2) Begin a journal, either hand-written or online. Attempt to write every day. If writing every day seems like a burden to you, simply begin by writing one thing for which you are grateful every day. I promise you that your journal will evolve, and in the meantime, you are practicing gratitude.

3) Create a sacred space for yourself to begin a meditation practice. Practice the proper meditation posture from the Dalai Lama so that it feels comfortable to you. Also, play around with what may assist with reducing your mind-chatter (sound, guided meditation, breathwork). You can begin with a five-minute meditation goal each day or whatever works best for you.

Solitude is about going within ourselves in our created space—to gift ourselves a moment. It is that quiet alone time for Self-Reflection, to form a Journaling routine, or to develop our Meditation practice. Solitude provides the space where we can finally be honest with ourselves, where we can map plans, and where we can dream of all we can be. It is also space where we can work through parts of our being that we may need to recognize and then let slip away, for they no longer serve us.

My advice for you is to incorporate solitude into your days. Even the extroverts among us need this space to develop into the best version of ourselves. Allow yourself the gift to stop. Solitude, and all the practices within it, can provide us with space to heal. This healing space is where we discover the balance of light and dark, of our masculine and feminine nature, of life and death. Find your balance within the sacred space that you create for yourself.

Chapter Four

Mother Earth

Our planet, Mother Earth, is an amazing gift to all of us. Simply being outside in nature can awaken us to her beauty and make us feel more alive. When we can immerse our physical selves within her essence, with our hands in her soil or our bodies in her waters, we are granted the benefits of her energy. When we walk among her trees, we breathe in their oxygen and feel the energy of the forest. When we simply sit in her presence, our senses become alive from what we see, hear, smell, and touch—and perhaps taste. Depending upon where we live, our experiences with the planet will be different. And for those lucky enough to travel, we are blessed with experiencing other wonders of Mother Earth outside of our daily lives.

As I began down my path, I determined I needed to create time for myself in nature. I began with a wooded trail near my house. Mostly I went alone. Part of this mission was to face my fears as well. I do not have a dog, so I worked on confronting my fears of being alone in the woods. I worked on breathing in the oxygen released by the trees, not jumping five feet when a chipmunk crossed my path or scurried in the leaves, and in finding peace by myself. I continued this exploration to a local state park with a small five-hundred-foot bluff. It may not be a high elevation, but it provides a beautiful vantage point of our bay and surrounding farmland. A nearby place to sit and take it all in. The other place I would go was the ocean. Often, I would go and put my feet in the water, but other times I would just sit on a rock and breathe in the salt air. I also realize how fortunate we are in Maine to have immediate access to such natural beauty. The beauty you have access to may be slightly different, but I guarantee you can find the natural beauty in your surroundings that speaks to you.

I did not grow up calling our planet Mother Earth. As kids in the '70s and '80s, you could not get us inside. We preferred being outside. Yet, as a whole, we did not acknowledge or give gratitude to the planet. In fact, the everyday person did not always treat the planet so well back then. There was a naivety, an ignorance about how many people treated the planet. I remember trash being tossed out of car windows like it was a commonly accepted practice. Houses with a nice embankment on their property made for a convenient family dumping site. Thankfully, the majority of us have progressed from that point. Of course, we are now in the midst of a global environmental crisis due to many factors. Although we can get involved in environmental action groups to help make a difference at a larger scale—and these things need to happen—it is what we can all do within our space on the planet that can help create change as well.

A first step is becoming aware of how much the planet provides to us. Until we make ourselves aware, it is too easy to simply exist—and take our planet for granted. It behooves us all to form an appreciation for nature. Immerse ourselves in nature when the opportunity arises. In doing so, we become connected to her essence.

And then we get into doing our individual part of taking care of Earth. At any point in time, most of us can do better—if we are honest with ourselves. The important thing is forming an awareness and taking the steps forward to be more respectful of the environment. Often it is easy to think of our homes as self-contained units that do not have an impact on some of the larger issues, but most of us do contribute our share, and then all together we can have a larger negative effect on Earth. Although many of our acts may not be intentional or malicious, the results do have an impact. Recycling, reducing single-use products, moving to reusable water bottles, and buying locally raised food are a few quick improvements we can easily fit into our lives. Becoming aware is a first step, and then we keep stepping forward.

Mother Earth also holds a history within her. We are hardly the first to walk these lands. There is the history of those who have protected her and revered her. As you explore the lands, be aware of those who walked before you. Be respectful as you walk in nature. Often their spirits can remain, especially the Native peoples. Their presence should be acknowledged, gratitude given, and an offer of healing to the spirits. Not too long ago, we went for a short hike to a waterfall on Penobscot Nation land. As we walked on the ledge above the river, I could *feel* their presence. I acknowledged, gave gratitude, and sent healing. It is about slowing ourselves to open our awareness and paying our respects. If we know an event occurred on the land or if we sense it, send not only gratitude but offer healing to the land and the spirits.

In this chapter on Mother Earth, we will touch on the benefits of Connecting with Mother Earth, the Gratitude we should have toward the planet, and why it is so important to form an Awareness of Our Impact. Throughout this book, you have and will see many moments in which nature plays a vital role in our journey to discovering the truest version of ourselves. Forming a connection to the natural world is a key component of our journey.

My hope for you is that you will develop a deep appreciation for Mother Earth. When spending time in nature, we bring our awareness to the present to fully appreciate her wonder. In being fully present, we develop gratitude for what we are experiencing, witnessing, and receiving. Let us open our awareness to how we can contribute to her well-being and let us begin stepping forward in our appreciation for all which she provides.

Connecting with Mother Earth

Mother Earth is a powerful source for us humans. She offers us so many opportunities to connect with her for our well-being. She is powerful medicine—for both our physical and our mental health—from the medicinal herbs she produces to the peace we feel by simply being out in nature. Aside from the sights, sounds, and smells of nature that give us this peaceful feeling, there is more to it! There is the direct physical connection to Earth herself, which provides the most extraordinary opportunity for healing.

When I was first introduced to grounding, I must confess that I considered it simply another practice in this new nontraditional world I was entering. I thought, *I will do it, but does it actually do anything?* Little by little, I felt the need to get outside and connect. Back then, I was not aware it was being marketed in the mainstream media as grounding or earthing. To me, it was simply making the connection to Earth when a person feels unsettled or disconnected, along with forming a spiritual connection to Mother Earth.

And then, I was introduced to the science behind it.

First, what is earthing or grounding? It is connecting to Earth's natural electric charge by walking barefoot on conductive surfaces such as grass, soil, gravel, stone, or sand. If we do not have ready access to nature, there are conductive products available to create our grounding means indoors.

Studies are showing that earthing or grounding can have an immediate or rapid positive impact on inflammation, pain, stress, blood flow, and sleep—to name a few of the benefits. And all we need to do is walk barefoot outside for a few minutes every day.

Now, with that said, I may be analytical, but science is not my strong suit. Let me attempt to put this in layman's terms; however, I recommend you do your own research as well.

The earth is struck by lightning and soaks in the sun's radiation, which affect it electrically and provide Earth with a renewable source of free electrons. This gives Earth a natural negative electron charge.

Then there is us. Due to our disconnection to the planet, we have an electrical imbalance in the form of a build-up of positive charges within our bodies. Let us think about how infrequently most of us walk barefoot on the ground, how often we wear synthetic soled shoes that act as an insulator when we do go outside, and more than likely, how often we are immersed in electronics and are inside—either at home, work, or school. Electrically, we are a mess.

By earthing or grounding, we are allowing a transfer of free electrons from Earth directly into our body. These super-hero negative electrons enter our bodies and neutralize the naughty positive charges that may have been creating damage to healthy cells—often in the form of inflammation, the demon cause of many illnesses. The negative electrons are our immune system's reinforcements! Restoring the intended electrical balance within our bodies. Maybe we call them our *resistance*!

Of course, I am not a doctor, so please do your own research here. This is more to give you a snippet of information to pique your curiosity. The man pushing this new age wonder is Clint Ober, and you can research his journey in getting the medical and scientific community on board to the benefits of earthing.

Also, we have all heard of tree huggers! Make fun no longer. Think about the roots of those trees and how deep down into the earth they go. When the cold of winter comes upon many of us, that big tree in the yard may need a little squeeze! You will become grounded just as we ground our electrical systems in our homes into Earth as required by our local town and city code enforcement officers for safety purposes.

Mother Earth provides us with resources to not only reset our electrical charge but also to cleanse and purify our energy field. As we untangle negative or unwanted energy from ourselves, Earth has the ability to transmute those energies. We can simply place our hands on the earth and release those energies with intention and gratitude…and breathe. We can access the cold, salt water of the ocean to clear ourselves as well. Whether hesitantly walking into the water or swimming in its depths, the brisk ocean salt water will clear our energy field and refresh our being.

As we walk down this path, we will be introduced to clearing ourselves with other modes as well. The first clearing tool I was introduced to was using sage to smudge. It was recommended to me by people at an estate jewelry shop after purchasing a ring. Having no idea what I was doing, I bought two packs of two bundles of sage. More than enough to clear a single ring! Sage, or a piece of palo santo (considered holy wood) are likely to be the most common means for the general population on this journey. It is the smoke released as we burn them that does the clearing, along with intention. Find a practice that works for you. There are many techniques and interpretations out there. Find what speaks to you.

Another clearing tool from nature is crystals. Collecting crystals is one of the first steps on the path for many of us. There is a lot of power residing within these beautiful little stones and crystals that we are collecting. We will discuss their qualities in an upcoming chapter. In the meantime, and as with all things coming from Earth, have gratitude for them. They are a gift from our planet.

Gratitude

Having gratitude in our lives is important. Gratitude is a higher-frequency act, feeling, emotion. When we live in a place of genuine gratitude, that frequency returns to us—just as acts of love, kindness, and compassion do. Although we may think having gratitude is mostly a response delivered toward people or for the acts of people, gratitude for Mother Earth and all she provides to us is important as well.

As we would in teaching children, we must instill in ourselves the practice of gratitude toward our planet. Two great places to begin practicing gratitude toward Mother Earth are to be aware of and acknowledge all she provides to us, and the second is to give back to her—to help her heal.

This planet that we are privileged to live upon is part of us. We are all one. The earth, the land, the oceans, the trees, the animals, and us—we are all one. I can still feel silly at times as I verbally give gratitude—and that is okay. Early on especially, I felt like I was faking what I was saying. Not because I did not understand we should have gratitude—it just felt outside of the person I was. I simply did not acknowledge gratitude in such a way. But, awkwardly, I continued. As part of my morning ritual, which we discussed in the Self-Healing chapter, I give gratitude every morning, and first up on the list before anyone else is Mother Earth. And every day, I feel the love and gratitude a little more deeply.

In addition to Mother Earth, we should have gratitude for all the plants and creatures who reside on her. The symbiotic nature of all living things makes this fascinating factory work. You need only look at our bees to appreciate this. What would our world be without bees and their power of pollination? How about our trees? Trees absorb the excess

CO^2 in the air and release back oxygen for us to breathe. Along with providing homes to birds and animals, trees provide a plethora of other benefits to us humans.

How many people do we know who began gardens during the 2020 pandemic? For those of us who joined in the fun or were already on the garden train, how absolutely captivating is it to watch a seed transform into a plant, which then produces food for our family or household. Couple creating a garden with composting our food wastes to help feed the plants and allowing them to grow better, faster, stronger while reducing the waste sent to the transfer station. This is a perfect place to have gratitude to Mother Earth. The exercise of gardening connects us to the planet, teaches where our food comes from and what is going into it, and often creates a new household project. In doing this, we are helping to reduce the pesticides placed into the earth on big farms and reducing the transport needed to get the food to us. We just need to get our green thumbs working.

Another simple act of gratitude is to plant a tree. Here in Maine, we are extremely fortunate to live where we do—surrounded by trees; however, this is not the case for many areas in the world. If we feel having a tree planted in an area of deforestation or wildfires would be of greater benefit than in our yard, we can simply donate to the cause. In late 2019, two online personalities, Jimmy Donaldson and Mark Rober, challenged their online followers and fellow creators to raise twenty million dollars in two months to plant twenty million trees through the Arbor Day Foundation—and they did it! These are young people calling other young people to action. Twenty million in two months! This taught many young people the impact that they can have together on the planet. I read one donation for a dollar, where the child posted, "My tooth fairy money." How awesome!

So, gratitude. We all need to show gratitude to Mother Earth— ideally in both forms. We are in this together. Acknowledge and give gratitude as if she were a person—the same with the plants, trees, bees, and all other creatures. If it feels strange at first, no worries. You will feel it more each time you acknowledge, and it will bring your awareness to the moment, of being in the present.

A final lesson of gratitude and appreciation for Mother Earth is when we discover something with such beauty in nature that we feel the need to "have it." When we take from the earth, we should acknowledge with gratitude. A beautiful shell at the ocean, a rock along a hike, wildflowers from the field. Give a simple nod of gratitude or another way of acknowledgment that you may learn along your journey. The ultimate sign of gratitude may be in leaving the treasure where it is so others may share in its beauty as well.

This world of awakening brings the important things into focus, and having gratitude for Mother Earth is a great step in acknowledging all that she does for us on this journey.

Awareness of Our Impact

This portion of the chapter is about bringing an awareness to each of us regarding the impact we have on the planet. It is not meant to hit every topic or issue, but to create a beginning for many of us. It is meant to help us consider our impact on the planet and to further advance where we are now in our awareness.

With no ill intention, the reality is that most of us do have a negative impact on our planet—unfortunately. Becoming aware of the far-reaching impact of what our daily decisions can have on the earth is a step in the right direction of changing those ingrained practices and making us more conscious of our actions. Once we open ourselves to the awareness, we can begin to make more positive decisions for the earth in our daily lives.

Unfortunately, Mother Earth has not always been treated as she should be. We can discuss the impact of the Industrial Revolution, deforestation of the rain forest, global warming, or the myriad of other issues created by our population over time. Since this chapter is not about solving all the issues in a few hundred words, let us discuss our individual contribution to the issues and a handful of changes we can make now.

A good place to begin (or continue stepping forward with our current practice) is by becoming aware of our carbon footprint and what we can do to reduce our impact. We mentioned earlier in the chapter a few low-hanging items, which we can all begin today; however, we all likely need to work on additional changes as well. To reiterate, let us begin with losing the single-use drink bottles and opt for reusable bottles instead. Easy enough. For that matter, let us lose as many single-use products as possible. It happens occasionally, of course. But by raising our awareness, we think twice. And thinking twice is incredible progress for the overall population. Think twice about the purchase we are about to make. Do we *need* it? One way to approach purchases is to ask ourselves, "When I am done with this, where will it go?" You know the super cute stuffed animal we really want to purchase for a loved one—where does it go when the person is done with it? We cannot donate it. It goes to the landfill. Ouch!

Think twice about the clothing we want to buy—where will it go when we are done with it *or* could we buy it from a consignment shop? Think twice about the food we buy at the grocery store. Could we buy locally to reduce the transport necessary to get the food to our table? For that matter, what food are we eating? Are we willing to join the wave of Meatless Mondays to help reduce the carbon impact created by livestock? So many things before we even get to home energy audits or automobile usage. There are plenty of resources out there on the internet where we can go to find a list of the changes we can incorporate into our lives to reduce our footprint. Become aware and act, even with small steps, and begin to think twice.

Considering that approximately 70 percent of Earth is made up of water, taking care of our oceans, lakes, rivers, streams, and any other water source is vital. Since my kids were little, we have always gone to our small local beach to pick up sea glass. Occasionally, the "sea glass" would be too sharp—not enough time in the ocean. Eventually, it warranted explaining when clearly freshly broken beer bottle fragments were washed up on the beach. Treasure or trash? I suppose we were fortunate not to have more than "sea glass" washed up. This new awareness triggered my daughter to organize her first beach cleanup for us when she was around seven years old.

Yes, awareness around the world is increasing, and we are in times where many of our waterways are being cleaned up, but there is still more to be done to correct many of these impacts from our past. Although we may be able to fish again in certain rivers and lakes where we once were unable to do so, it is still unsafe to eat the fish from many of these water sources or necessary limits have been placed on the number we should eat, due to high mercury levels or other cancer-causing toxins found in the fish. Pesticides and fertilizers remain an issue as runoff makes its way to our water sources as well. Not just from farms, but from our own yards. This is without even getting into what we are dumping into our oceans.

Awareness. It can be uncomfortable at times, but when an issue becomes personal, that is when change is more likely to occur. Awareness of where the products we purchase and consume originate, where they end up, and what impact they leave behind. Perhaps we even concede our green lawn to an environmentally and creature-friendly garden instead.

To discuss the creatures of our planet, I have chosen the story of our bees. We likely all recognize bees as a vital creature for our ecosystem. Our plants depend upon bees for pollination. Unfortunately, as a population, we have genetically engineered our crops, often practice monoculture, use pesticides to keep the crops "healthy," and finally, we use "harvest aids" to expedite a bountiful harvest. When our bees go to work, they pick up all these poisons and bring them back to the hives. We are killing the bees or greatly altering their lives—and this does not even get into the impact these poisons are having on our human population.

How do most of us contribute to this? Let us look at two of the big crops, especially in the United States: wheat and corn. We Americans love our bread, pasta, cereal, and crackers. Carb overload! Do we need to consider our consumption of these products? Sure, we do. Not only the environmental impact but the impact of consuming these products ourselves in great quantities over a prolonged period. We are consuming the pesticides and fertilizers ourselves. Think of the demand created by your household multiplied by millions of other households. Most of the corn production in the US is used for livestock feed, which delivers us to our demand for meat—a long topic and environmental impact story for another day. The foods we consume create a demand for products from these big farms. We become enablers. It is easy to forget how a product gets to the grocery store and the impact it leaves in its wake as we innocently grab a product off the grocery shelf or cooler out of convenience.

Awareness is really the first step in becoming an active participant in caring for our planet and the creatures on the planet, including ourselves. Becoming aware, stepping forward in our awareness and our efforts, and beginning to think twice.

Exercises

1) I would like you to look up grounding or earthing on the internet. There are a few articles and videos that offer the scientific research behind earthing and provide findings from supporting studies. With the facts behind you, get outside to ground with Earth—barefoot. If getting outside barefoot is difficult, consider purchasing conductive products. The bonus of getting barefoot outside is being in nature—breathing in the air, stilling our mind, and letting go. Do this as often as possible.

2) Whether you live in the country or the city, I am going to challenge you. Find yourself a planter of some sort. It does not have to be deep. Buy a packet of lettuce seeds—whatever your preference. Sow and grow your plants inside or outside (if it's warm enough). The plants will grow quickly with minimal care. Whenever you want lettuce, you will have access to fresh lettuce for salads, sandwiches, and smoothies. It will taste better than store-bought, it will be on-demand with little or no waste, and you will not be contributing to the use of the large plastic containers in which lettuce is often sold. Have fun and enjoy!

3) Challenge number two. Yes, things happen; however, I want to challenge you to eliminate plastic water or soda bottles from your life for one month. Buy yourself a nice water bottle and let that be your water

lifeline. After one month, I want to challenge you to a second month—and so on. Think twice and make a difference. It is easier than you think.

Some of the Mother Earth chapter may have come across as a little heavy. Although confronting some of the realities of what is happening to our planet *is* heavy, it does open our awareness to the changes needed to be made by the population, as well as by us individually. Making a personal connection to nature and having gratitude for all that Mother Earth provides to us is a gift and helps to open our awareness.

My advice to you is that you form a connection to Mother Earth by getting out in nature, connecting with the earth's beauty, and creating a deeper awareness of how we can all take care of the planet. Remember to think twice as you make purchases. Consider where the product or packaging will wind up after use. Reduce or eliminate the number of single-use products you consume. Think twice. The planet takes care of us so well—from the negative electrons we bring into our bodies by standing on her to the oxygen her trees produce for us to breathe. In the end, we all need to have gratitude, offer healing, and take care of our planet.

Chapter Five

In the Present

Being in the present. The words seem so simple. What are the chances, as you transitioned to this chapter or just picked up the book to begin reading again, that your mind was still in motion as you began reading the words? I know I find myself doing this all the time, and then having to go back to read a few sentences again. I often chuckle to myself, especially when I am reading about a topic such as being present. Well, they say the first step is awareness.

One of Merriam-Webster's many definitions of being present is "at or during this time: *now.*" Again, the words seem so simple. Yet the step from awareness to incorporating being present into our lives can feel gigantic! How and where do we begin?

Being in the present is one of those premises that is easier said than done for most of us. I was taught to begin small early in my journey. Bring our mind to what we are doing in the small moments—even with seemingly mundane household chores. The lesson was about breaking down these household chores into points of gratitude and finding joy within the moments. It could be doing laundry, making dinner, cleaning up from dinner, or washing the windows. If we have gratitude for the clean water, the food, the clothing, the house, and the many other items for which we should have gratitude, it changes the experience. It changes our energy, our outlook, and the outcome. We find joy in those routine tasks. Discovering joy in these moments brings peace, and peace brings calm. Realistically, applying this mindset to household chores may take a little practice on our part, but we begin.

We should realize this way of approaching life applies to time spent with others as well. Being in the present and being mindful of our moments can impact others around us. I cannot think of any more important place to practice this than when we are with children. I have seen it in the eyes of a child when someone is looking at their phone instead of giving their full attention to the child who is excited to share. Truly, the same goes for us adults. We like to receive a person's undivided attention when we are sharing, yet how are we about giving our undivided attention to others? I am guessing we all have a little room for improvement.

What about our thoughts? We could all likely use a little help here as well. How do we keep our thoughts in the present? It is easy enough to say that we need to keep our focus on what we are doing now, but achieving that focus is another thing. Many of us struggle with keeping our thoughts on what we are doing in the present. Instead, our thoughts get mired in our past or our future—neither of which we can fully control. The reality is we cannot change the past for it is done, and the future has yet to occur; however, the future is created by the small moments of the present. Being in the present can positively impact our future.

In this chapter of being In the Present, we are going to discuss opening our Awareness to living our life in the present, form Gratitude for those people, places, and things in the present, and develop Practices for being present.

My hope for you is that this chapter will speak to you. So many of us need to work on living our lives fully in the present as opposed to living in the past or future. It is a much healthier place to reside. It allows us to learn to appreciate the small details of life and have a happier existence. Living in such a way will likely draw others to us, for they will feel our energy and our rising consciousness as we discover the joy brought to us by living in this way. Again, joy brings peace and peace brings calm. To begin, we must practice bringing our awareness to all moments with gratitude.

Awareness

My partner makes light of how easily I can be distracted. The expression "squirrel!" holds true here. Not only can I be distracted by physical, tangible things, but even the intangible things can take me away—a thought, an idea, a vision. I am a marketer's dream and always have been. I am the food industry's easiest prey. I know I am not alone here. We have become a world of distractions—unfortunately. The good news is we are becoming aware of how toxic this world of distraction can be. And, although I just made light of being distracted, we all need to work on reigning in our minds for our own health and our relationships as we proceed through our lives.

Distraction from the present also has the capacity to wreak havoc on the state of our mental health as we stress about our past and worry about our future. An interesting thought as we flashback through the times in our lives where this may have held true. Ironically, my daughter has me reading the young adult fiction series *Shadow and Bone* by Leigh Bardugo before it is released on Netflix in spring 2021. As I was tweaking this chapter one last time before editing, I read the following from book three, *Ruin and Rising*, "We had too much time walking with nothing to do but think, and there was no safe place for my thoughts to wander. The past was full of horrors, and the future left me with that breathless, rising panic." There it is! Even our fictitious heroes struggle to remain in the present with their thoughts.

We live in a world of angst and a world attempting to control our angst, often in ways not good for our soul. Of course, I am not a counselor, a psychologist, or a psychiatrist, and I am definitely not downplaying the world of mental health. What I am suggesting is that it is going to be a tough road ahead if we try to fix the whole world—so let's not try in this moment. Let us begin with the person for whom we are most accountable, and that is ourselves. Let us not attempt to do this is in one day and expect miracles. Let us simply begin.

To begin is to attempt to be present in our moments. We are not going to change the past. We all wish we could erase or modify a thing or two, but we cannot. It is time to move forward. We all would like to dream of the future…or sometimes avoid the future if there is something uncomfortable there; however, this moment we are in is not the future—just yet. Interestingly, we can block time in the present to make a plan for the future or to begin taking the steps to make that future uncomfortable situation less uncomfortable. This can be a productive use of the present that makes our future better.

We have all heard of people finding their groove in what they are doing, of being in the zone. This can be achieved through athletics, business opportunities, gaming, or many other situations. Even as kids, we could sometimes achieve this high—maybe shooting baskets in our yard or on one golden afternoon with the pogo-stick! The theory of achieving the high can be interpreted in a few ways; however, the crux of the interpretations is that when a person is *in the zone,* they are neither in the past nor the future. Instead, they are intensely focused on the present. In some cases, reaching this level of performance can come from a person achieving a balance of focus (awareness) and effort, along with their skill set, allowing the person to apply less effort yet perform at a higher level—again, finding the zone. The thought is that what the mind achieves, the body will follow. Be it peace of mind, focus of mind, or ease of mind, the body will follow. And here is the kicker, allegedly we can apply this to our everyday lives.

Let us give this a test. While writing this portion of the book in 2020, I went on my first mountain biking ride in almost thirty years, and, honestly, I had never done anything at this level previously. The paths in places were a foot wide, in others there were rocks (a lot of rocks), and there were tight turns—some of the ride was simply struggling uphill and in other places, we were going downhill at speeds beyond the comfort level with which I began the ride. The light went on. I needed to watch what was approaching every second. It was over three hours of constantly being in the present or what was quickly approaching my path in the extremely near future. I did not think about the past or the future, beyond the rocks in front of me. Was I *in the zone*? Perhaps on the periphery of the zone. Although I was neither in the past nor the future, and I had the awareness of focus, I was likely exerting more effort because my skill level was less than necessary for the activity. A nice try.

Regardless, have I incorporated these interpretations into my daily life since? Not with any consistency. It is retraining how we approach life. It is not easy, but we begin. Awareness of living our life in the present is a first step in bringing this sense of ease to our everyday life.

Being a list-making person, and assuming you come from a similar list-making school, lists do help with the awareness challenge from a conceptual standpoint. We can time-block our workday to lend some structure for us, which then allows us a better chance of being in the present in those moments. Then, during time with family and friends, time alone in nature, or completing simple chores, attempt to be present in what we are doing and with whom we are having an experience. Having an awareness and attempting to be present in our moments may be the first step, and then we continue to step forward.

Gratitude

Yes, gratitude, again. Being in the present and gratitude go hand in hand. If we think about how fortunate we are to be experiencing whatever experience we are having in a given moment, we are better able to stay in the present.

Once again, nature is the most amazing place to have gratitude and be in the present. It can be as simple as stepping outside in the morning and inhaling a long breath of (hopefully) fresh air. In that moment, we can be grateful for the breath we are taking, for the oxygen we feel filling our lungs, for the sun rising to begin the day, for the warmth of the sun on our face, and for the connection to the earth as we, perhaps, feel the grass under our feet—as those negative electrons race into our body to stabilize our internal electrical system. So many moments of gratitude in a simple act—within the present. When we are fully present, we can break down such a simple encounter with nature into that many points of gratitude.

How about our interactions with others? Our connections to people, loved ones or strangers, are so important. Gratitude is not only about giving *thanks* when we receive a material gift from a person. Being in the moment with a person, giving them our full attention makes a human connection beyond what most of us experience in every-day life. It does not matter if they are a child or an adult, people crave human connections, and those connections are far more important than any material gift. More difficult in a time where we wear masks; however, have you ever made eye contact with a stranger and smiled at them for no reason? This simple act can change a stranger's day and our own. Be grateful for acts of love and kindness and be present enough in our awareness to extend these acts of love and kindness to others. And be present enough in the moment to allow them to feel our full attention.

There are many daily rituals where, if we stay in the present with them, in gratitude, the experience changes completely. We can find this with any of the tasks we mentioned at the beginning of the chapter; however, let us look at the task of doing laundry—likely not high on anyone's list. The next time we wash, dry, fold, or put away our laundry, attempt to remain present with the tasks. Do not see them as chores. We are not internally complaining about doing the laundry as opposed to someone else in our home doing the laundry. Just be present. Be grateful we have enough clothing for ourselves and our family, that we have clean water to wash the clothes, and that we have machines to do the washing. Sounds a little silly perhaps, but it works. In the same vein, when we eat the food that we prepared for dinner, be thankful for how the food arrived on our table. Eat more slowly to savor the flavors. Be grateful for the sustenance going into our bodies. Slow down, be present, and have gratitude for every seemingly small detail.

Maybe a bit more challenging to incorporate into our lives is remaining in the present when things are awkward or uncomfortable. However, if we break it down, is it the present that is uncomfortable, or is it the future situation that could result from the action in the present? Remember we talked about stress resulting from past events that we cannot change, and worry created by future events that have not yet occurred. If we remain in the now, living a life being fully present and having gratitude while letting go of the past, won't our future be a little less stressful…a little less anxiety-ridden?

You say, "Tina, but sometimes I do not want to remain in the present. There is a person/situation/event in the present I would rather avoid— let alone be grateful for."

Fair enough—so how do we get around this situation, because the present is truly the *best* place to reside? What if we were to look at the situation from the perspective of someone who is observing us in this unwanted situation? What if we were to look at this situation as an uninvolved, unattached bystander whose function is to determine what it is we are to learn from the ghastly situation in which we find ourselves? Would doing so remove our emotional connection to the situation? Would being the unattached spectator allow us to have gratitude to the situation for teaching us a valuable lesson we can carry forward on our journey? A little deep, but a possibility.

Friends, what we are separating ourselves from in the above scenario is our naughty little ego—the part of each of us that gets in our head and hijacks our thoughts, often our reasonableness, and our precious rational thinking. If we can separate ourselves from a situation, remove the emotions, and not react, then we remove the power of our ego. For our ego does not like us to reside in the present. Our ego wants to torment us over the past and the future, "I can't believe I/she/he/they did that!" or "I don't know how I can possibly get this project done in time." Let us attempt to step outside of ourselves, removing the power of our ego. Be present, and not only be grateful for the lessons we learn but be grateful for our newfound awareness.

A quick story to help illustrate this point. A friend called me recently to vent about an ex who had contacted her. She is on the awareness train already but still needed to vent. In stepping outside her reactionary self, her ego, and portraying the role of a neutral bystander, she was able to quickly remove her emotions by concluding the call was likely triggered by the ex's own insecurities as he processed his own shortcomings in a situation. There was no need to fall into her instinctive reactionary defenses—there was nothing to defend. It was his issue! Life moved on with a little gratitude for no longer being in the relationship, and although there was still a small trigger, her awareness allowed her to step back and process quickly.

In this day and age, much of being present and having gratitude is about slowing down. We are constantly on the go and typically attempting to multitask. Regardless of what we have been taught, multitasking is not a feather in our cap. It is simply a concept created by our population to justify our lack of attention, at least in my opinion. Begin to slow down and give focus to individual experiences, people, and tasks. Be in the present with them and have gratitude for what each moment shares with us, teaches us, or just is.

Practice

Now that we understand opening our Awareness to being in the present, along with the power of Gratitude for all we experience in the present, let us put these new tools into practice.

A fantastic place to begin is with our senses, and what better place to work with our senses than in nature. We are coming off our chapter on Mother Nature, so we already realize the magic held within her. She is going to assist us in practicing being fully present. The byproducts of this exercise are enhancing our senses, deepening our connection to the planet, and triggering our intuitive abilities and creativity. Pretty awesome stuff. The exercise is simply to go outside and find a place to sit. It can be in our yard, the park, a trail, the ocean—anywhere where we feel comfortable. Sense by sense, focus all our attention on what we are experiencing through hearing, seeing, smelling, touching, and tasting. I am not telling you to lick the ground, but do see if you can taste nature. This was an exercise from *The Medicine Way* by Kenneth Meadows. The intent of the exercise was more about attuning to our senses, but it plays beautifully into bringing ourselves into the present as well.

In addition to helping us build an awareness of living our lives more fully present, nature is an incredible teacher as we practice the art of connection. The natural world provides us with the space to see things for what they are in their simplest form—a flower, a rock, a tree, a creature. Can we learn to appreciate something or someone for what or who it is in its truest sense?

As we tend to do with people, we instantly begin labeling things without allowing ourselves to have a pure experience. We walk into a beautiful garden and we are drawn to the pretty pink flowers of a shrub because pink is our favorite color and the shrub is an azalea just like the one we had growing up; therefore, it is our favorite shrub in the garden. We have not allowed ourselves to simply be in the moment. To simply appreciate natural beauty as it is.

Now let us go ahead and look at this premise with people. We walk into a room and approach a person we have not previously met. Before any words are spoken, we can feel the energy of the person. We can feel their vibe. And then we introduce ourselves and begin asking questions. What do you do for a living, where do you work, where did you go to school, what kind of vehicle do you drive, where do you live? Label, label, label, label, and label. Now we have constructed a whole opinion of the person that may or may not match with the *feeling* we had about them when we walked up. We have defined the person as to whom we think they are without actually knowing the person. It is human nature in today's world. Likely, we cannot simply stand there in silence either, but it an interesting point to think about.

I want to touch again on the conversation about ego, since we are talking about people. When I use the little trick of stopping my reactionary self and viewing the unfolding scene from the perspective of an outsider, I feel like I have been given the answers to a test. Try it! Sometimes we end up simply not responding, sometimes it is responding calmly, sometimes it is walking away...or not responding to a text. Regardless, not being the crazy, reactionary, needing-to-be-right, or defensive person simply feels good. It saves so much of our energy. Staying in the present helps to diffuse our ego.

In the end, our everyday lives are full of moments to practice being in the present. Household work, gardening, cooking, and time with family. We all need to make a concerted effort to be present with these moments. Given my personal issues with attention and my list-making nature, time-blocking my workday brings about the best chance for me to focus my attention on a matter. If I know I have one hour to complete a task, I am better about holding my attention on the task. I try to build in "attention breaks," knowing I need to derail occasionally to keep the balance. We each know what mental head games we must play with ourselves to achieve success. Figure out what you need to do to keep yourself in the present as much as possible.

Exercises

1) Practice being in the present. Pick one time today to keep your attention in the now. Just one moment. It can be giving a friend 100 percent of your attention while talking with them on the phone *without* folding laundry while you talk. It can be thinking about the ingredients you are using while cooking—their smells, how they got to you, the gratitude for them. Pick whatever you want. Now stay in the moment. Perhaps tomorrow you try for two moments.

2) Try the exercise discussed in the Gratitude section. When you wake up, step outside and take a deep breath. Now break down each moment of gratitude within that one act. Greet the morning sun with gratitude, whether it is visible or not—you know it is there. Think of the oxygen filling your lungs, feel it within you. Be grateful for the sun or rain or snow welcoming you on this morning. Feel it on your face. Give gratitude to each moment as you greet the day. Maybe try this as you step back inside to make your morning tea or coffee as well.

3) The next time you are confronted with conflict, take a deep breath to allow the space to step outside of yourself as the unbiased observer. What are you meant to learn from this scenario? Is this your issue, or does the issue belong to the other person? Stay present, remove emotion, and diffuse your reactive self. Does it warrant a reaction or even a response?

I want to quickly touch on a point I made earlier in the book. We are all on our journey. We have already covered a lot of topics in the first few chapters of the book. You do not have to incorporate everything into your practice or into your life at this moment. Think of this book as a buffet. Sometimes we sample a few different foods, sometimes we pile our plate high with one particular item striking our fancy, but we can always come back for more. This book is not meant to be everything for you. You will need to research some topics further for scientific justification, to learn more about a practice, or to have an experience with a topic—to find what makes sense for you. Design your own journey.

With that, we wrap up our chapter on being In the Present. My advice for you is to open your awareness of the present and step forward into it. Having gratitude for all your moments, for the people in those moments, and for the experiences in those moments will bring a sense of peace to your existence. Find your joy in the present. The ultimate goal is to live within the present; however, becoming aware and finding moments to practice being in the present are incredible steps on your journey as a conscious individual.

Chapter Six

Filling Our Canoe

One of my early lessons from the shaman was that I needed to fill my canoe—that each of us needs to fill our own canoe. What does filling our canoe mean? It means creating our own space where we can be all we are—have our own interests and hobbies, build our knowledge, discover our truest self, and evolve into the happy person we are meant to be. Fill our canoe with who we are.

Many of us fall into the label trap in life, as we brought up in the last chapter. Think of the labels either we place upon ourselves or others place upon us. I have been my parents' child, my sister's sister, my workplace's salesperson, my own boss, my children's mother, my partner's…lady friend (we struggle with naming this label), and so it goes on. While identifying within our labels, many of us often either jump into another person's canoe or welcome people into our canoe, which can result in our losing a bit of the essence of who we are.

Two labels where it can be particularly tricky to maintain our own canoe are *parent* and *partner*. As a parent, we load the whole family into one canoe. Often, we may even lose ourselves in our roles of mom or dad—forgetting who we once were. We need to encourage our children to fill their own canoes as they grow. Help them develop their healthy independence and teach *us* to let them move forward on their journey. The other tough relationship is with our significant other. Oh, how we like to cozy into a canoe truly built for one! We think, *look how much we have in common.* And, in a co-parenting relationship, what happens to the relationship when the children leave the house? Chances are we are different people than when we brought these little bundles into the house. Have we filled our canoe enough over time to be our own person in a healthy relationship with our rediscovered spouse when the kids leave the house?

Although we should each be in our individual canoe, we can still do things with our loved ones and friends to experience these *things* together. We simply meet one another on the river, do our joint *thing* for a bit, and then hop back into our own canoes allowing each of us to maintain our essence.

I recently read Gisele Bündchen's book, *Lessons: My Path to a Meaningful Life.* The book has been out for a couple years and I have been curiously drawn to it—more than just because I am a Patriots fan and she is Tom Brady's wife. Gisele has accomplished extraordinary and inspiring things in her life and continues to be a positive force for environmental causes particularly. I was pulled to the end of the book where Gisele tells the story of marrying Tom. She had discovered a poem to use at their wedding ceremony by Kahlil Gibran in the chapter on Marriage from his book, *The Prophet* (1923). I believe it is a fitting poem to share here as well, especially as it pertains to holding onto ourselves within a relationship.

> *You were born together, and together you shall be forevermore.*
> *You shall be together when white wings of death scatter your days.*
> *Ay, you shall be together even in the silent memory of God.*
> *But let there be spaces in your togetherness,*
> *And let the winds of the heavens dance between you.*
> *Love one another, but make not a bond of love:*
> *Let it rather be a moving sea between the shores of your souls.*
> *Fill each other's cup but drink not from one cup.*
> *Give one another of your bread but eat not from the same loaf.*
> *Sing and dance together and be joyous, but let each one of you be alone,*
> *Even as the strings of a lute are alone though they quiver*
>   *with the same music.*
> *Give your hearts, but not into each other's keeping.*

For only the hand of Life can contain your hearts.
And stand together yet not too near together:
For the pillars of the temple stand apart,
And the oak tree and the cypress grow not in each other's shadow.

Although we have people who share this journey with us in life, each and every person is on an independent, unique journey. To live this journey fully, we need to allow ourselves to discover the essence of who we truly are and our purpose in this lifetime.

The shaman had another related lesson for me regarding our role as a parent. He reminded me that our children are connected to us, literally for women, by the umbilical cord. The physical cord is cut at birth; however, the symbolic cord remains. As we fill our canoes and rise to be all we are meant to be, our energy is fed to our children through this cord, and they too will rise.

Through this chapter of Filling Our Canoe, we will talk about Interests and Hobbies, the gathering of Knowledge, and discovering what brings us happiness Within Ourselves. This chapter is about bringing our awareness into being our own fulfilled person.

My hope for you in this chapter is that you experience an *aha!* moment. Losing a little of ourselves happens over time, like erosion. It is time for all of us to reclaim ourselves, learn more about ourselves, and grow into the whole person we love…in our own canoe.

Interests and Hobbies

The simplest way to fill our canoe is by finding the things we love to do, the things that bring us happiness. In many ways through this journey, we have the opportunity to discover what makes this evolving us genuinely happy. Again, what an exciting opportunity.

I go back to the 2020 New Moon Intention list that I began just prior to the new year and decade. One of my intentions was to add to my canoe. I actually made a small canoe out of clay two or three years ago. I keep it on my bookshelf in my nook to remind myself to focus on filling and maintaining my canoe. Each month when I wrote out my intentions in 2020, stepping them forward from the previous month, I added a new interest or hobby to the list. Both writing this book and my fifty-mile bike ride were items I added in 2020. In many ways, this is similar to what parents do with young children—as perhaps our parents did for us. We introduce them to many different sports and hobbies when they are small so they can find what they love to do. Unfortunately, we often get caught up in the routine of life and forget we should do this for ourselves as adults as well.

My partner's sister is the best person I know for trying out new interests. She may only do some of them for a short while, but in the meantime, she has pushed herself outside her comfort zone and given the new interest a try to determine if it is something she would like to incorporate more fully into her life. Not continuing a practice is not quitting; it is discovering what makes us happy and letting go of the rest. It is okay to release things from our canoe.

My sister has done a similar thing with her spiritual toolbox. As she began her journey, she became certified in Reiki II, Akashic Records, and Access Bars therapy. She then went on to become certified in equine Reiki, became Reiki III certified, was certified in restorative Yoga, and recently completed her two-hundred-hour Yoga teacher training. Mix in her intuitive prowess, and she makes magic happen in her *she-shed* she had built. She has followed her own intuitive guidance in assembling her spiritual toolbox to place in her canoe.

A few times in my life, I have attempted to incorporate more fully the things I enjoy in my life. In true list-lover fashion, I had to set them as goals: each month I would read one book or attend one show when I lived in Boston (pre-kids). We should try out new things or reincorporate past loves back into our lives and use whatever tool or mental maneuver works for us to place them into our canoe.

Pushing ourselves outside our comfort zone is good practice. It makes us feel alive and provides a feeling of accomplishment. We love to see this in children. Why not in ourselves? After twenty-five-plus years of not placing my bottom on a bicycle, aside from a stationary bike, my partner reintroduced me to biking a few years ago. During the summer of 2020, I became inspired after watching a documentary of an unathletic man who pushed himself to run an ultra-marathon. Since I do not like to run, I decided I would bike fifty miles instead, and then tied it to turning fifty in a few months. Having not biked much in 2020, I needed to train. After a quick six weeks of training, my partner and I did the fifty-mile ride last weekend on September 19, 2020—exactly six months to the day before I turn fifty. Would I place biking in my canoe now? Yes. Although we biked together on the long rides, I mostly trained by myself during the week. As a novice road rider, I pushed my comfort zone about being alone on quiet roads and composing myself on busy streets. As I write this, I am about to stop so I can go on a quick ride before jumping into the day. I will put the bike in my canoe—for now—and occasionally I will meet my partner to ride together before we resume our journeys in our own canoes.

Of course, there are creative hobbies for us to consider, as well. We will get into more details about creativity in another chapter; however, let us touch on it briefly here. For many of us rational-minded people, we understand the intuitive, right side of our brain may not be quite equal to our left, more logical side. Yet here we sit—needing to fill our canoe and knowing creativity is a healthy part of being. I have quite simply determined in my life that I must put ego aside and realize my execution will not match my expectations when it comes to creative endeavors. Accepting perfection is relative, and my interpretation (or ability) is just fine. Life is not perfect. Through this journey, I have discovered that, although my mind sees precision, say in a landscape painting, my abilities are more impressionistic or abstract. I have come to accept and appreciate the perfection of the imperfect order.

Try new things, push your comfort zone, be okay if things do not look textbook "perfect." Simply find what you enjoy doing. You may try out a new hobby only to learn that it does not make your heart sing. It is okay to simply let it go. Part of the fun is in discovering what makes our heart sing. This could even mean unleashing your creativity. It does not have to make sense to anyone except you—and even that may not be necessary, as long as it makes you happy.

Knowledge

Fill your canoe to the brim with knowledge—it will not sink the boat, I promise. The definition of knowledge is "facts, information, and skills acquired by a person through experience or education; the theoretical or practical understanding of a subject." Read, watch, and listen, but also experience. One of my loved ones once told me, with all the confidence in the world, that he could fly a helicopter. We then discussed the emotions, the adrenaline, the outside factors involved when you are flying a helicopter in the real world versus virtually. It is similar to a conversation Robin Williams had with Matt Damon in *Good Will Hunting*. His character explained that we can read all the books about Michelangelo, but until we stand in the Sistine Chapel and look up at the ceiling, we have not fully experienced its beauty, nor do we fully understand—I paraphrase.

As we fill our canoe, remember to fill our minds with knowledge through books, podcasts, documentaries, videos, *and* experiences. As we venture down this path of self-discovery, we are likely going to be drawn to expanding our knowledge—it helps us justify. For me, it began because I did not know much about this new world I was entering!

In fact, one of the best practices to have come back into my life during my journey has been reading. It is fascinating which books present themselves along the way. Books we may not have considered will land in our lap and, sure enough, we will be able to pull out a few points that resonate with us at a moment on our journey. Autobiographies and memoirs can be surprising. They tend to show up and may not initially make sense as to why, but there always seems to be a nugget there. Transformational books will suddenly appear in two or three places before we awaken to the sign and then grab a copy. Used books can find their way into our hands when they make sense as well. Personally, I feel like I could sit and read nonstop. Be aware and open. Books are like their own path on this journey. Follow the book path as it unfolds itself for you.

Documentaries and other streaming videos have been another source of knowledge. When we feel a draw, we can simply begin to scour all the streaming sites to see what grabs us. Over time the sites will make recommendations based on our viewing history. Listen to what speaks to you. I am always pleasantly surprised by the new nuggets delivered to me. Podcasts are another source of great information.

And experiences! Learning through others, as well as participation in activities, makes our world real. Just remember there is the theory of a matter, and then there is the reality of the matter. Before we build something up too much or, contrarily, discount it too much, have an actual experience with it. As I mentioned in the Self-Healing chapter, my entry into seeing a shaman was as a curious skeptic. I am forever thankful for the knowledge brought forth in my time with him. Had I relied solely on what I thought I knew, I might never have had those experiences. Same with the new or full moon ceremonies. I could read about them, but it is a whole different experience to hold ceremony, especially with a group.

On this path, we will all pick up a book offering us a new meditation, a new journey, or other aspects we can add to our practice—even words or routines to add to our daily rituals. The easiest way to see if it "fits" is to include it and see if it feels right for you. Once again, stay fluid with your expectations of yourself and this journey. Things evolve and we grow. Trust what feels right to you in any given moment. This thirst for knowledge seems to intensify as we progress on our journey.

Lastly, many of our new experiences can be coupled with the new interests and hobbies with which we are experimenting. What better way to determine if a new interest is to our liking than to give it a go— have an actual experience with it. For many of us coming from a similar place of thinking, knowledge is where we can help ground ourselves. Knowledge can feel almost tangible to us. As you move forward, build your knowledge base through education and experiences. It is a fascinating journey for sure. Watch where your knowledge takes you. It is a journey in and of itself.

That Which Is Within Us

Now that we have begun to fill our canoe with interests, hobbies, knowledge, and experiences, what else is there? Maybe it is purely what resides within each of us: our truth, our opinions, our desires, and our dreams. We will stop short of labeling it as who we are, because do any of us actually know who we are—without using labels? Ultimately, what is it, within these things residing within us, that makes us happy?

This journey, which we are all on, is about stepping forward as the truest version of ourselves. Stripping away all the labels and ideas of who we thought we were or what made us happy, especially the material items, is part of the process. Becoming our truest self and stepping into our truth takes work and dedication. Most of us have been programmed our entire lives onto a path that does not necessarily nurture our souls. Removing the layers to expose the raw us is intimidating and can make us feel vulnerable at times. It is time for all of us to uncover our truest selves and discover what makes this version of us happy.

I found I often stepped further toward my truest self when I kept parts of my journey to myself. Without judgment of others (real or perceived), I could step forward more freely. It allowed me not to question what was unfolding as much—solitude was my safe zone. All I needed to hear was confirmation of this fact in a piece I was reading, and within myself and my world, I retreated.... or rather, I progressed into my journey. Others I know did not isolate to the same degree, but embraced their tribe. That simply did not feel fully my path. Although I would still gather with the group, I trusted my lone wolf path was the proper place for me to grow. You will need to determine what feels right for you on your journey. A combination of the two is likely the healthiest option. The goal is to allow ourselves the freedom to develop into our truest selves.

In the safety of our canoe, what opinions do we hold that make us happy? At times, things we hold as strong opinions or get upset about are mere trivialities in life, so we must not get completely lost in our opinions; however, having an opinion and allowing it to evolve as we do can bring self-awareness and happiness to our canoe. Maybe it is as simple as what we would eat for dinner if no other person's opinion came into play. Maybe it is a little bigger, and our voiced opinion could have an impact on a job or a relationship in our life. As we step forward into our truest self, into a new level of happiness, realize we can begin to question our preexisting opinions within ourselves. Offer ourselves the chance to have a new opinion on things within this evolving self. Allow ourselves to create a new level of happiness.

Being in our own canoe allows us to consider what we desire or dream for our lives. Perhaps certain things felt seemingly far-fetched previously, or we may consider new things brought forward since beginning this journey. Some of these new desires may be a stretch from our prior selves. Remember, we are the only ones who put limits on what we can dream possible in our everyday world. We should be excited, while maybe a little nervous, to stretch ourselves. Consider what would make our hearts sing. Could we set ourselves on a path to attain a new desire or dream as we fill our canoe?

What it all boils down to is what makes us happy as we step toward the truest version of ourselves. Let us fill our canoe with those things!

Exercises

1) Remember the intention list I keep talking about? The site www.foreverconscious.com had a twist to the basic intention list for the new moon leading up to 2020. I love this. Make a list of ten intentions you wish to manifest if you have not already. Now create a symbol to represent each intention. It can be anything you wish to use as representation. Now draw or paint these symbols on paper or canvas. Create a piece of artwork out of these symbols that you can keep in your workspace, on your altar, or another place where you spend time during your days. When you glance at this artwork during the day, you will be reminded of your intentions, and you will be inspired to step forward with them.

2) Head to a bookstore, library, or online shopping and let yourself be drawn to whatever pulls you. Read the reviews online or browse through the physical books. You may not understand why you chose a certain book until you read it, and you may not read it until a future date, but add it to your library. You will feel the pull to read it when appropriate. Begin your book journey. Begin to build your new library.

3) Find a space of solitude for a little quiet introspection. Allow yourself to dream. Consider your life. What is something you could add or change about your life that would bring you the most joy? The one requirement is it cannot be about anyone else except you. What could you add to your life that you passionately feel would bring you joy? Now ask, "How do I incorporate this into my life?" It does not have to be overnight, but give yourself time to sit with this idea of the new addition. How can you put this item of happiness into your canoe—whether it is a feeling inside, knowledge, an experience, a new hobby, or a new interest?

In my last year or two in Seattle, I really got the bug to incorporate as many activities as possible into my world. I made list after list—an all-encompassing list, which I then pared down to various daily lists. I began playing soccer on two co-ed teams, attended ballroom dance classes twice a week, did yoga, took various classes at the club, golfed, played a little racquetball, enrolled in an adult swim class, and partied too much (still in my twenties). My days were packed. If I had to guess, I was searching for something as I was nearing thirty. What I was not was *aware*, and what I did not do any amount of was *self-reflection*. And so life moved along until I was ready to begin this journey. We may see little glimmers in our lives; however, all of this begins in earnest when we are prepared to walk our path.

My advice to you as you evolve on your journey and work on filling your canoe is to remember our canoe is purely for us. We have many friends and family whom we love, but they should have their own canoes. It is fine and fun for us to tie up next to their canoe to participate in something together, yet we should each go back to our canoe. As we fill our canoes, fill them with our interests and hobbies, knowledge, and all that is within our being that makes us happy. And remember, it is okay to remove things from our canoes as well. Certain items, experiences, and even people come into our lives for moments along our journey—to provide us with what it or they were meant to provide us in that moment. Letting them go only means they taught us what they were meant to teach us, and we learned what we were meant to learn from them.

Chapter Seven

Crystals and Stones

Likely you have already found your way to a crystal shop, a metaphysical store, or a rock and gem show. You are not alone here. Crystals and stones seem to be the equivalent of dipping our big toe in the spiritual awakening waters. We may not understand or need to understand the draw to them in the beginning—aside from the simple fact that we like how they look. Perhaps we read the little description, which often comes with them, and the meaning resonates with us for that moment.

The urge to collect these beautiful products created by our planet is often a way for us to take our first little step. We can go into the stores and meander around checking out other things, but the crystals and stones simply feel like where we should begin, for they feel safe. Or maybe it goes back to allowing ourselves the feeling of participating in this journey on which we are embarking, and the crystals and stones are a quick and easy entry—perhaps less intimidating. Purchasing a crystal or stone here or there makes us feel like we are beginning to participate.

My kids and I began going to one particular holistic and gift shop as we entered our new phase of life. We would each look at the crystals and stones and select two or three that either spoke to us directly (grabbed our attention) or whose description we liked. Our windowsills, dresser tops, and shelves became bejeweled with crystals and stones. We would often carry them in our pockets, and we got matching amethyst point necklaces. Regardless of whether any of us embarking on this path believe crystals and stones actually do anything to help us early on, sometimes simply hoping there is a chance offers peace enough. The manager of the store got to know us because we were in there so often. Between the energy of the crystals in the shop and her intuitive and kind nature, the shop became a safe haven for us when we needed to be tethered. It has now been a few years, and life has settled. The crystals and stones remain in my kids' bedrooms. They may not be as active with the crystals now, but they are still there.

My collection has evolved over the years. Occasionally I would pick up what I would consider a medium-sized crystal, or my magical ladies would gift me one. Crystal points were randomly added to my collection without understanding their healing powers. My sister and friend made a couple trips to England and gifted me with stones from there as well. And, more recently, my partner has gifted me with a few incredible pieces over the last couple of years. As with anything that comes into my collection, I may not fully understand its purpose in the moment, but I know the reason will arrive eventually. My own crystal purchasing has waned a bit, and that is okay. I likely have what I need for this moment in my journey. I will feel the call when and if that changes.

Another fun place to incorporate crystals into our lives is with a pendulum. I have always leaned toward an amethyst pendulum, but we all find what works for us. Believe it or not, I typically do not trust my intuition—I say with sarcasm. Using a pendulum takes that pressure off us—even though it is our intuition that makes the pendulum work. If I must be honest, I formed a little pendulum addiction there for a while. A slight intervention later and I eased up. Occasionally, I will take it out, but I try to sit in stillness for a moment before calling in the big hitters! So what is a pendulum? Quite simply, a pendulum is a crystal connected to a chain. We determine, with our pendulum, our *yes* and our *no*. For example, *yes* is a circle and *no* is back and forth (or it could be the reverse for you). *I don't know* typically will stop the sway of the pendulum in its tracks for me. And then, you ask questions. A couple of years ago I was guided to write out an alphabet grid and used the pendulum with the grid to spell out words. I had a blast with this early in the journey. My advice would be to remember the goal is to eventually trust your intuition.

Finally, a great place to bring crystals and stones into our lives is with jewelry. There are so many talented jewelers out there now, and we really do not have to break the bank to purchase a piece or two. We can simply let ourselves be drawn to what calls to us. My sister and I both replaced our engagement rings with beautiful pieces we purchased at an estate shop. The rings we chose were perfect for the healing journey. Mine disappeared about a year ago, and her ring found its way into her jewelry box, but both rings did their job for us in that moment of our journeys. Have fun with this one! And this is not just for the ladies. Everyone can find super cool pieces out there as well.

In this chapter on Crystals and Stones, we are going to discuss A Little Crystal Knowledge, how crystals relate to our Chakras, and the healing and manifestation powers of Crystal Grids.

My hope for you in this chapter is for you to learn a little bit about the origins of the crystals and stones to help create a reverence for them. Open yourself up to the wonders of the crystals' healing powers and their connections to our energy centers, our chakras. Learn to eventually trust your intuition in designing your own crystal grids. More than anything, simply form an appreciation for the natural beauty of crystals and stones and enjoy the process of learning more about them. Have fun with your adventure!

A Little Crystal Knowledge

As we ready for a discussion of using crystals and stones in our practice, let us first have a quick Crystal 101 lesson before we dig into the rest of the chapter.

Now that the idea of crystals has been planted within our brains, we are all likely pining to head out to a shop this weekend to begin or expand our crystal and stone collection. Being our rational-minded thinking selves, maybe we should brush up on our crystal knowledge before we take to the stores.

Every crystal shop, either brick and mortar or online, has its own sourcing practice for obtaining crystals and stones. Perhaps those little crystals and stones we purchase from a bin with the descriptive piece of paper are simply purchased in bulk. Maybe the shop owner is more involved in the acquisition of the larger or unique pieces by forming relationships with more vetted wholesalers. Whatever their practice, this piece of Earth that we are contemplating purchasing has been excavated by miners, sold to wholesalers, sold to retailers, and perhaps, sold and resold through different owners. Many hands have been involved in getting this crystal or stone from the earth to us. As a result, we will likely want to clear this crystal or stone of any energies it could be carrying from its journey to us. Possible ways to cleanse the crystal or stone are to smudge it with sage, run it under cold water (if that is appropriate for that particular piece), hold it over a flame or smoke, or clear and charge it in the light of a full moon.

Going forward we may want to cleanse our crystal or stone again when the need arises. Also, we can charge our crystal or stone by placing it on a charging plate (we can find them in all the normal crystal places), placing it on a larger piece of cleared crystal (typically some sort of quartz), or placing it under the light of a full moon. There are additional ways, but these will get us started.

So this beautiful new crystal we just purchased from the store—what is its origin? I personally love a shop that will tell me in what country or region the crystal was excavated. Nonetheless, it is easy to forget sometimes, when we really want to purchase a particular crystal, that the extraction of the crystal from Earth is a business. Like anything, sometimes the business may not always do things the right or safe way. As with many things on our journey, it is about building an awareness. At times, our little crystals could be a side gig resulting from large mining operations for more precious materials. Other times, our little crystals are the gig. As the demand for crystals increases, we should be aware and encourage ethical mining practices and sustainable protocol from our supply chain. In the unregulated crystal industry, this may mean purchasing from vendors who maintain a supply chain as close to the source as possible. Unfortunately, in most instances, we still will not know the entire story of a crystal's journey to reach our hands. Once again, we begin to form an awareness of our impact resulting from the demand we create.

Now a little science for us. How exactly are these crystals created? Mother Earth is a constantly changing planet. If we go back to middle school science class, we learned about the layers of Earth and tectonic plates. We learned how crashing plates create mountains, and how fault lines in the plates can create earthquakes and volcanoes. There is a continuous heating up and cooling down of rocks and minerals within Earth's layers which allow the planet under our feet to recycle itself. Our planet is in continuous movement. This constant movement, heating up and cooling down, eruptions, and pressure over time help create these beautiful crystals and stones. It is all quite spectacular.

Why are crystals part of this journey? We touched on vibration briefly in the Self-Healing chapter. Basically, everything is energy—whether it is us or the crystals on your windowsill. The crazy part is we are the unstable ones. Our emotional state is easily influenced by outside factors making our energy unstable. We may begin our morning feeling great because a nice stranger paid for our coffee while we were in line. Our energy is vibrating at a high frequency. We get back in the car and continue our trip when the car in front stops suddenly, and we slam on our brakes sending our hot coffee into our lap. Our energy becomes hot along with our lap. Crystals, on the other hand, are stable. Partly due to their geometric shapes but also because they are fixed, their vibration cannot be influenced. Their vibrational frequency is very stable and powerful. With a bit of deductive reasoning, we understand that we, the unstable vibration, can therefore be influenced by the crystals, the stable vibration. Interesting. This is before we even get into the colors of the crystals!

Chakras

Time for everyone to pull out a Chakra 101 book or bring up a website. In this journey of self-discovery, our chakras are an essential part of self-healing and are integrated into many aspects of the overall journey, including crystal use.

First, the most basic definition of our chakras is that they are our energy centers in our body—and remember we are all made up of energy. Additionally, in Sanskrit, chakra means wheel or disk. Our chakras are basically spinning wheels of energy located at seven points of our body, and when they are open, they allow the life force energy to flow—the universal energy. When people discuss and work with chakras, they typically begin at the bottom and work their way up. The following list contains the chakras; the location of the chakras; how each particular chakra is associated with our mind, body, and spirit; and the color with which each chakra is associated. We will get into more details with the colors in a moment.

1) Root: located at the base of spine; associated with our primal senses— our sense of safety, security, and survival, along with a connection to earth (being grounded); associated color is *red*.

2) Sacral: located just below our navel; associated with attracting the pleasures in life and our emotional bodies, including our creativity and sexual energy; associated color is *orange*.

3) Solar plexus: located in the stomach area at our diaphragm; associated with confidence in our personal power—our beliefs, principles, and self-esteem; associated color is *yellow*.

4) Heart: located at our heart; associated with unconditional love and compassion—without fear or judgment; associated color is *green*.

5) Throat: located at our throat; associated with communication and finding our inner voice to speak our truth; associated color is *blue*.

6) Third eye: located at the center of our foreheads slightly above our eyebrows; associated with our sixth sense of intuition, self-awareness, and increased observation; associated color is indigo.

7) Crown: located at the top of our head; associated with surrendering to Divine guidance—being one with all; associated color is *violet*.

Now the fun part. Many (many) of us are a bit of a mess in our energy centers. Our chakras can be a bit muddied up—possibly even blocked. When this happens, our life force energy cannot flow properly...and we feel it even if we do not know what "it" is. Many (many) of us have some severely stuck energy inside of our bodies at various energy centers, and it will take work to move the energy. To begin to move the energy, we need to do some self-healing, along with clearing. A great tool to help clear our chakras is with—you guessed it—crystals and stones.

Crystals and stones are made up of a beautiful rainbow of colors—as are our chakras. Crystals and stones are made of energy vibrating at certain frequencies—as are our chakras. When our chakras are muddied up and not functioning properly due to life's challenges, we become imbalanced. By aligning corresponding crystals and stones by their colors to our chakras, these stable sources of vibrational frequencies help to rebalance our energy centers back to their proper frequencies. Smashing! The even crazier part is that we often intuitively know what we need. When you visit a crystal shop, take note of which crystals and stones you are drawn to in that moment and what the corresponding chakra is. You will be pleasantly surprised by how you truly know what your mind, body, and spirit needs. Another fun side note is to check this phenomenon with fruits and vegetables as well. Often what our body craves aligns with the needs of our energy centers—match up the colors.

As we begin using our crystals for clearing our energy, a good starting point is to simply allow ourselves to be drawn to the crystals that call us. As I mentioned earlier in the book, my kids and I would carry around the crystals and stones we liked on certain days or those whose message resonated with us. We did not know the connection to the chakras at the time. Simply do what feels right. There is no need to force anything. At some point, it may feel right to begin to place the corresponding crystals on our chakras as we look to clear our energy centers. I used to lie flat on the floor and place the crystals on the appropriate chakras. I would then breathe in their energy while focusing on each chakra independently in sequence—beginning at the root chakra. Evolve and discover what practice works best for you. There are many sources for you in books and online. As always, sample from different sources to assemble a practice unique to you.

Crystal Grids

As I mentioned at the beginning of the Self-Healing chapter, using crystals for grid making will evolve when you are ready to incorporate them into your practice. I remember not being able to conceive how people designed grids, how they knew to put certain crystals where they put them. I looked at it more like a work of art being designed. That was the extent of the thought I gave to grid making until grid making entered my evolving world.

First, what are crystal grids? Crystal grids use the energies of the crystals, along with sacred geometry, to create an amplification tool to manifest intentions. Depending upon a person's intention, different crystal combinations can be used, along with different grid designs.

There are plenty of websites offering templates for creating crystal grids for various purposes, and this is a valid place to begin. There are also crystal shops and online vendors who assemble crystal grid kits where you will receive the template and the crystals to produce a particular grid. I want to challenge you to eventually listen to your intuition and begin to sense which crystals to place in your grids as well.

When you feel ready to create a crystal grid, consider what your intent is: healing, healing for a particular chakra, health, love, abundance. As you learn the attributes of the various crystals, you will know which ones make sense for a particular intention. Using various types of crystals combines their energetic powers. Grid making is another way of putting our intentions out into the Universe, and many people will write their intentions on paper to go along with the grid. As we visit various websites on creating crystal grids, we will learn we need to clear our space as we begin to make our grid. We need to hold our intention with each stone we place; some say to begin on the outside and work our way to the center as we place the crystals and stones, and the center stone should be a more significant piece, such as a crystal point. As always, my feeling is for you to do what feels right to you. I was not aware of these procedures initially, but my intention was true.

Here is how crystal grids entered my realm. Crystals came into my world over time, along with a handful of medium-sized crystals. During a trip to the crystal shop, I was drawn to a fluorite point, but I did not know why. Weeks (or months) later, I *felt* the need to move the fluorite point to the center of a small table in front of my bedroom window, and then surround it with three medium crystals from my collection in the shape of a triangle: a marshmallow crystal, a cactus (spirit) crystal, and green calcite. This healing grid remained for a few months; however, I was guided to create a second grid on the shelf under the healing grid, and this second grid would change about every couple of weeks. It began with a quartz-based grid to help charge or amplify the healing grid. If I was working on certain chakras, I would find the bottom grid would change to support that. Once I opened to accepting and did not attempt to control it (too much), I simply changed the grid as I sensed it was time. Soon after the first healing grid went into place is when I was guided to begin my meditations in front of the grid. I had not meditated previously. I am a turtle and move from point A to point B at a slow pace. My journey presents me with these gifts at a pace that allows me not to freak out. Small crystals became medium crystals became a grid became two grids became a meditation center became a chakra clearing space—all in due time. None of this journey happens overnight.

So like everything on this journey, we each need to determine what works for us. If you want to kick-start your healing, and grid making feels right for you, by all means, research grid making, and maybe even buy yourself a kit. Each of us evolves over time, and you will know when it is the right time to begin trusting your own intuition in this practice. And being the people we are who enjoy a little structure to things, having a template on how to build a grid is a great way to begin stepping forward on this path. Or you can be like me and let your guides drag you along.

Exercises

1) Do some quick online research on which crystals correspond to your seven chakras. On your next trip to the local crystal shop, handpick a crystal for each chakra and begin to develop a connection with them. Small crystals are fine to use. Begin to bring your awareness to which crystal calls to you on any given day. Perhaps carry it in your pocket for the day to give focus to that particular chakra. When you are ready, consider using them to begin clearing your energy centers.

2) Treat yourself to a piece of jewelry. When the time feels right, find yourself a shop—with new or used jewelry. When you see the right piece, you will know. It will call to you and will typically be your size. It was not until after I purchased my first ring on this journey that I discovered jade helps heal and protect our hearts—exactly what I needed in that moment. Remember to smudge the piece of jewelry before you begin wearing it.

3) When you are ready, give grid making a try! Think about what you would like help in manifesting. It could be healing, wellness, abundance, goals. Search online for a grid design to support this desire. If you have the needed crystals, fantastic. If not, you can go to the crystal shop, or you can simply improvise. Do what feels right to you. Trust your intuition. Grids can be simple or complex. Sometimes we try to make things more complicated than they need to be. With your grid in place, meditate in front of it and see where things take you. Enjoy the journey!

As I write this book, all my crystals and stones and my existing grid are currently located in a dresser drawer. At some point in 2019, I was guided to take this beautiful silk material, which I had purchased two years earlier to make a tapestry for meditation but had never done so, and place it inside an empty dresser drawer. On the material, I placed the grid, along with a little Buddha statue my partner had put in my Christmas stocking a few years back—and off to the sides are all my other crystals and a singing bowl gifted to me by my kids. When I meditate, I pull open the drawer, carefully light a candle on the floor under the center fluorite point, and sit in front of the drawer for my morning meditation. When done, the candle goes back on top of the dresser, and the drawer gets pushed in. I am still not certain why the drawer happened, but I will say that my crystals are clear and dust-free for my morning meditations. My larger crystals remain out on display.

I hope this chapter on Crystals and Stones has left you with the bug to incorporate them into your new practice. They are such captivating creations, and their abilities to help realign us are real. There are many online vendors these days; however, I encourage you to get to a crystal shop to experience them in person as well. The energy in these shops will often have you leaving the shop feeling a sense of peace.

Find yourself a chakra book that speaks to you and learn about your energy centers, their flow, and their corresponding crystals. Begin incorporating crystals into clearing your chakras, along with having some fun with grid making. And, above all, have gratitude for your new crystals and stones. Not only gratitude toward Mother Earth for creating them but to the individuals who helped bring them to you as well. Lastly, clear your new crystals and stones as you begin incorporating them into your practice—or as you simply enjoy their beauty.

Chapter Eight

Self-Care

As with many stepping-stones in this book, aspects of the Self-Care chapter can be found in other chapters as well, especially the Self-Healing chapter. Self-care can seem like one of those luxury practices, when we should all be incorporating self-care into our daily practices.

What exactly is self-care? Self-care is really defined by each of us—in what brings us comfort and joy for our mind, body, and spirit. In many ways, it is how we can pamper ourselves. There is some overlap with the Self-Healing chapter for sure; however, my interpretation is that self-care is more about taking care of ourselves in the present and in a gentle way.

Now, you may ask yourself, "How are we going to include everything mentioned in this book into a daily practice? There is not enough time in the day." True enough. The fact is, we do not. I am five years into my self-discovery, transformation, awakening, self-awareness journey, and I most certainly do not fit everything into my daily practice. Certain items that are part of our spiritual evolution may find us along our journey, and then they may leave us eventually; other items may be added to our daily checklist; and then there are simply those items that we may need to schedule—for they may take a little more effort to incorporate into our day, week, or month.

Self-care feels like a continuously evolving practice for ourselves and one that allows us to restore balance to our being. One of my early additions to self-care was in deciding I needed to take better care of my health by becoming more consistent with vitamins, as well as finding natural ways to handle any health concerns. In doing this research, I discovered a miraculous way to handle the new hot flashes that were visiting me multiple times a day. Whatever the combination was which I concocted, it worked quickly and to my pleasant surprise, my hot flashes went away almost immediately. As I write this, I have been hot flash free since May 2018. For anyone who has hot flashes, has gone through hot flashes, or knows anyone who is or has gone through hot flashes, eliminating them is a life changer. Beyond self-care!

It is interesting how people define their self-care. One practitioner reminded me of the need to indulge our senses with softness. She recommended taking a warm bath and curling up with a soft blanket. Recently another practitioner asked me what I was doing for myself, and when I merely sputtered, he reminded me that we all deserve to take a day or two or three to simply cater to ourselves. And for many of us, getting outside to ground and breathe is a necessary part of self-care.

We are going to approach this chapter by looking at how Our Senses can bring peace to our being, how taking care of Our Health creates a strong vessel, and how Our Spirit can reach higher vibrational frequencies through love and kindness, compassion and healing, inspiration and gratitude. Within each of these categories are many opportunities for self-care. As always, we each have the ability to define our journey as we see fit.

My hope for you is that you look at this chapter as food for thought and helpful reminders on how you can make your life a little softer, a little kinder, and a little healthier. You know what makes you happy and brings peace to your world. Do those things more! You deserve it! By caring for yourself, you are creating a vessel of positive energy. The world needs every positively energized vessel! As we rise, those around us will rise.

Our Senses

Back in the Mother Earth chapter, we discussed using our senses to open our awareness. In this chapter, we will focus on bringing softness and calm to our senses as part of our self-care.

Catering to our senses does not have to be time-consuming or expensive. Coming from our realm of linear thinking, perhaps we have only considered bodywork in our self-care routine, a routine that tends to be on the pricier side of self-care but is a bit more in line with how our world mostly operates. Does that make sense? Massage, especially, tends to be a largely accepted practice for everyone. I had never truly opened myself to indulging my senses beyond bodywork until this journey. I assume I am not alone here. In the end, it likely does not matter where we are on the spectrum of catering to our senses. Chances are we could all take more time to pamper ourselves.

Let us begin with touch. When we feel the softness of a piece of clothing or a blanket, what do we instinctively do? We pull the item up to our face and rub it on our cheek. There is comfort in a soft touch. How about the water in a warm bath? Feeling the water surround and embrace our bodies brings about a sense of peace. How about human touch? One of my favorite things to do when my kids were little, and even now, is to gently rub their faces and watch them fall into a deep relaxation. The power of touch. Massage, facials, and other bodywork are all so important for this reason. In my mid-twenties I began going to a spa for my eyebrow waxing (once I realized I had an eyebrow "issue"). The waxing itself was not my favorite thing. What was my favorite was that the practitioner used essential oils to rub my temples after the waxing. My job was a bit busy and stressful, and for twenty minutes every other week, I indulged for a moment. The spa had relaxing music playing and would offer me tea or lemon water while I waited. I would have my session, and they would let me stay in the space for a few minutes afterward—similar to a massage. All of this for a simple eyebrow wax. I looked forward to it every other week. When I moved to Boston, it took me a few different establishments to find an esthetician who even came close to that Seattle experience—and she did not have the relaxing music or tea and lemon water. It was all about the touch—she rubbed my temples too.

For much of our day, we have the lights turned up, or we are looking into the lighted screens of our devices receiving a visual overload. How does our mood change when we turn off the lights, shut down the devices, and light a candle? Same room, but a completely different mood ensues. Even a dimmed light changes our mentality. Recently, I was home alone and decided to do some baking. I lit a candle and put on some chill music. I felt so at peace. The chatter in my head stopped, and I was more present in what I was doing. Finding a place we love and simply sitting is a great way to open our sense of sight as well. I find this in nature. Watching the clouds pass, the waves ripple, the various birds busying themselves, the leaves falling, or the animals scurrying around all bring me to the present and bring a sense of peace to the day.

The sounds with which we choose to surround ourselves can also change our mood. Like I said above, the music and candle combo, while I was baking, created such a soothing environment. We are all so "busy" in our lives that we do not stop to create this environment for ourselves often enough. I have gone through phases in this journey when listening to a certain hertz gives me a sense of peace, and hopefully helps align my vibration to what my body needs in that moment. I always love a little Tibetan or Native music depending on what it is I am looking to bring in for that moment. In the chapter on Self-Care, perhaps hard rock is not the best option for music choices—although it does have its place. And, of course, nature is a fantastic option. To simply sit and listen to the sounds of the natural world.

Smell is an interesting sense, isn't it? A smell can trigger memories that we were not even aware we were holding deep inside of us. If we are looking for smells that bring us comfort as we cater to our senses, we each need to think about what smells soothe our soul. I can name a couple for me. We live about a mile and a half from the Atlantic Ocean. The other day I stepped out the front door to the smell of the ocean in a light fog. I stood in the front yard and just breathed. It is one of my favorite smells in the world and makes me so happy. Another smell that makes me incredibly happy is the smell of my favorite tea steeping. The smell infuses the entire house. It is a mint chai tea made by a magical herbalist friend. Once again, the sense of smell can change our moods. Think about walking into our parents' house as a kid and how our mood would shift depending on the smell—think liver and onions versus chocolate cake!

That seems a good segue to taste. Remember, we are talking about comfort here. For me, some of my so-called comfort foods leave me feeling bloated and uncomfortable—so are they really "comfort" foods? In my life of trying to be healthier at certain points than others, I find the healthier I eat, the more I appreciate and enjoy the healthier food. To the extent of slowing down and savoring every bite. However, if we are talking about a singular day and allowing ourselves to indulge in food that is almost orgasmic in nature, personally I would go for a high-calorie, moist, dark chocolate cake. In my life, I have been fortunate enough to have experienced chocolate cake, which has made me reconsider if I ever needed a man again! I kid…sort of. Or…we simply go back to the above example and enjoy the comforting taste of the mint chai tea while cozying into a chair with a soft blanket.

Our Health

Our Health may seem like the most obvious place for self-care to many of us. It gives the feeling of being a more tangible practice. Once again, we are each going to place importance on the things that resonate the most for us individually. There are various forms of exercise for our health, there are services that help us maintain our well-being, there are products we use on our bodies, and there are the choices we make as to what we put into our bodies. While we will each form our own practice and investigate new endeavors, it can be helpful to bring things into our awareness as a reminder of what is available to us.

Exercise is an obvious self-care practice that we all should be incorporating into our rituals. And to be clear—I am *not* judging. Like everyone else, I will formulate a nice routine and pledge to never fall off the wagon again—until the next time I do. If this helps anyone, I will share with you that when I am most consistent is when I establish a reasonable goal and make a nice little chart where I can check off boxes. Lists win again! I have also found the exercises we dislike the most are the ones we are least likely to continue. Find exercises you enjoy and are more likely to do consistently. Finally, listen to yourself. People are full of advice, but what works for them may not be the exercise for you.

A great by-product of formulating an exercise routine is often better sleep, especially if you couple exercising with being outside. I sleep so well when I am physically using my body. And we all know good sleep is what makes this machine we call a body function at its best. We need sleep! Remember grounding from the Mother Earth chapter—another sleep aid, as is the miracle of magnesium. While you are at it, I recommend you look up the many benefits of adding a magnesium supplement to your self-care.

Next is what we put in and on our bodies. One of the first earthy-crunchy things I did on this journey was to make my own body lotion using organic ingredients. It is one of my favorite additions to my daily ritual. Along the same lines is adding essential oils to my day on occasion. Although I am a complete novice, I am realizing the potential that essential oils could have in my life at some point. Another new introduction for me is to herbal remedies through my spectacular herbalist friend. Our ancestors had it figured out. Even more simple is the importance of water. Again, I use my daily checklist to challenge myself with my water consumption. A little competition with myself works for me—maybe it will work for you too. I do this for everything I want to fit into each day: reading, writing, getting outside, meditation, water consumption, green consumption, exercise, and vitamins. I attempt to check them off every day. It holds me accountable for my own well-being, for creating and maintaining a healthy vessel.

As I mentioned in the opening of this chapter, my search for the right vitamin and mineral combination (and something to alleviate hot flashes) was part of my journey early on. Unfortunately, many of the foods we consume in our diets do not have enough of the vitamins and minerals we require, or we simply do not consume enough of the proper foods in our diets, and supplements do just that—they supplement the gap. I have my core vitamins and supplements that work for my needs, and then I add my precious topical magnesium. Do a little research to determine what may work for you. Some great websites offer helpful guidance for natural solutions. How great is it when we can figure out a natural solution instead of ingesting medicines?

Another means of being kind to ourselves via health may be through alternative health practitioners. These could include acupuncturists, massage therapists, polarity or Reiki practitioners, and chiropractors—to name a few.

Chiropractic care was a prelude to the start of my journey. Two months prior to the trigger that changed my life's trajectory, my back and sciatic nerve left me unable to stand for more than five minutes at a time. A chiropractor was recommended to me. I had definitely judged their services in the past even though I had never been to see a chiropractor. The chiropractor would not touch my back until he did X-rays so he could determine the root cause of my issue. During our first visit, he asked if I "took" anything, and I confessed I took a pain reliever every day for headaches, and allergy medicine had become a new addition during pollen seasons. He asked me to stop so he and I could understand my pain levels. I stopped. That was 2015. I have not taken any medication since, including pain relievers or allergy medicine—not once. A quick side note: The headaches were not due to my back. They were due to life. I would quickly learn as I began this journey that it is best to resolve the issue as opposed to masking the pain.

I know this is a long story, but I feel it is worth it. To continue. Although chiropractic care may not be on your radar, I am a born-again believer and place it on my self-care list. In fact, I go every week to this day. In addition to keeping me aligned, it has become an education in listening to my body. I know when I have been driving too much in a given week or not maintaining proper posture over the computer. I know when I am not releasing stress. I know when I begin a new exercise and my back is rejecting it. Look up *spinal nerve function* online, and a chart will pop up that tells us which vertebra is associated with which organ or function, along with symptoms that will show when vertebrae are misaligned. I would recommend looking at the Gray's Anatomy chart that provides more details and is easy to understand.

Our spinal cord is part of our central nervous system, along with our brain, and is protected by our vertebrae. Our spine is the superhighway for information between our brain and our body—and vice versa. When our spine is out of whack, it can impact our breathing, our digestive systems, our reproductive organs, and the like. Think of an electrical board or circuit board. Each wire (or nerve) heads to a different part of the house (or body). Keeping our spine in its proper alignment can alleviate many ailments people face and can allow us to get off some of the medications we ingest. For me, this is a critical part of my self-care. Why chiropractic care is not a common part of preventative medicine, I do not understand. Okay—that is my soapbox.

So many options for us to consider in taking care of our health as part of self-care. You are likely already incorporating some practices into your ritual and, if so, keep going. Keep stepping forward. If you know you could be doing a little more to take care of your vessel, look at this as an opportunity. Our health is a critical component of our journey. Be kind to yourself and your body.

Our Spirit

Catering to our spirit is not necessarily about developing our spiritual toolbox. We will get into that later in the book. By our spirit, I am referring to the softer side of our being.

This world of ours is in desperate need of love and kindness, compassion and healing, inspiration and gratitude. The fact that you are reading this book tells me you recognize this need in the world. And, although many of us are on this more awakened journey, we may need little reminders to provide these gifts to ourselves, as well as to others in the world—both to those we know and to those who are strangers to us.

Self-love and releasing judgment of self are essential self-care practices. They sound simple, right? Yet we can be our own worst critics. When we begin to release some of this judgment of self and form an appreciation of our minds, our efforts, our hearts, and even our bodies, we can begin to walk this life with more ease. No, I am not talking about all of us becoming narcissistic jerks. I am talking about loving who you are now—in this moment. Remember, our ego does not exist in the present.

And, as we embrace the love for ourselves, we should try to be love for others. Think how it feels when someone showers us with love. Put this energy out into the world. People will rise up. Offer simple acts of kindness to others and watch the responses. We should offer these loving acts without the need to post our good deeds to social media. That defeats the purpose and is an act to feed our egos. Be pure with our acts of love and kindness.

We have talked about gratitude in both the Mother Earth chapter and In the Present chapter, and it warrants a quick mention here as well. Having gratitude for all in our lives truly raises all of us up. It is that pause in life, keeping us in a moment, that allows us the space to appreciate all with which we are blessed. Continue this practice. It will change your essence.

In the Crystals and Stones chapter, we discussed that as humans we are an unstable vibration—emotions and experiences can change our vibrational frequency. With this, we should begin to surround ourselves with people with frequencies similar to our own, and ideally, vibrating at higher, more positive frequencies. Naturally, we will feel ourselves being drawn to these individuals. Be with these people who help us remain a more stable vibration. When we operate at a higher frequency, we project that vibration out into the world, and those higher vibrations will come back to us.

Allowing our spirit to be full of love can come through many means. All those items we put into our canoe will help us create a happier version of ourselves. Finding what lights us up, getting out in nature, finding our creative outlets, and being kind to ourselves and others—these will all change our lives in profound ways. As we rise, others around us will also rise. Our positive energy will draw in others.

Exercises

1) Give yourself the gift of an hour of self-care by creating an oasis for your senses. Indulge in a warm bath (touch) with calming essential oils (smell), while dimming the lights and lighting a candle (sight), playing

soft music in the background (sound), and savoring your favorite tea or perhaps wine or champagne (taste). If possible, ease yourself back into the rat race. Perhaps curl up with a soft blanket and a book for another hour!

2) Make your own body lotion. Here is a quick recipe I have retooled for my liking. Feel free to adjust for your own. In a double boiler melt the following: 1/2 cup beeswax, 1+ tbsp cocoa butter, 1/2 cup coconut oil. Once melted add 3/4 cup olive oil, and finally 1/2 tsp vitamin E oil. Pour into prepared jars. For me, this makes three four-ounce glass jars. Adapt the recipe as you see fit, perhaps adding an essential oil as well. I love this body lotion and use it every day.

3) Outwardly project kindness into your day. It does not have to be extravagant, just make it about projecting your positive energy out into the world—just by being you. Smile and hold the door for a stranger. Heck, simply look away from your device, smile, and say "hello" to a stranger. Give attention to someone who may need a little kindness. See how it makes you feel as well.

As we walk along this new path, self-care is really the essence of our transformation. Transformation of self is much of what we are talking about throughout this book. To recreate the framework of who we are. By attuning to Our Senses, attuning to our bodies and Our Health, and attuning to Our Spirits, we restore ourselves to the essence of our being.

My advice to you, to all of us, through this process, is to tend to our hearts. Our hearts are the gateways for our love and kindness, compassion and healing, inspiration and gratitude, along with our health. Our hearts hold or release our fears and judgments. Nurture all of them, except fears and judgment—we can learn our lessons from these two and then let them blow with the wind, for they do not serve us. Let us all discover our essence. Let us all be kind to ourselves and others while spreading love out into the Universe.

Chapter Nine

Our Tribe

Although tribe can have a Native implication, we will use the term here to refer to finding *our people*. The people who are on a journey similar to ours and are likely vibrating at a similar frequency as we are. These are the people who will understand our journey, people with whom we will share experiences, and people with whom we will form a spiritual connection. Now, with that said, finding this group of individuals can be like finding the right comfortable pair of shoes. We may try on a few before settling into the right pair. We may also outgrow our tribe or simply grow in different directions and need a change. This is fine too. Ultimately, it is we who must determine if our tribe fits our priorities and feels right for us.

When a group of like-minded individuals comes together, it can be a special feeling. We have talked about the assembly of people coming together for a new or full moon ceremony. There is a power brought to the gathering. However, keep in mind that my personal tribe can be different than your personal tribe even though we are part of a tribe together. This goes back to each of us being on a different journey and developing at our own pace. At times we may feel the need to participate in the new or full moon ceremony with our base tribe, while other times we may feel a pull to an individual we meet along our journey with whom we are to have a separate experience. We will each find our balance.

About a year or two into my journey, a loose-fitting tribe and those associated with my base tribe began work on a wellness center on a piece of land. Although I was on the journey, I did not have magic seeping out of my being quite yet and was not included in this magical endeavor—which was likely more about my not showing an outward interest. I felt a little left out, but then my own magic began occurring, and I got the feeling I was not supposed to be part of the group anyway. As my intuition became stronger, I would ask my guides if I should go to one of their ceremonies and the answer was always no. Instead, I became a tribe of one for the most part. A short time later, my sister asked if I wanted to go hold ceremony on the land with her since she had a client cancellation. I ignored my gut instinct and assumed this was a sign that I was to hold ceremony on the land with just her and not with the whole group. During our ceremony, we could feel the presence of the Native spirits. As we went to leave the land, my sister "was asked" by the chief, "Why did you bring her? She has her own tribe." Which I did. I was never supposed to be part of this group. And even as someone relatively new to this journey, I sensed every bit of it. This experience validated my need to trust my intuition, as well as releasing me from feeling sorry for myself—that I was left out. Those feelings were merely my ego at work. My point in sharing this story is to emphasize that the right group or tribe will present itself or will evolve for us. If it does not feel right, trust and remove our ego from wanting to be included. We know what is meant for us individually.

Finding our tribe is a great bonding experience. On this journey we will have moments of "Holy Schnikes!" and will feel the need to share what has happened with someone who will understand and not think we are crazy. The common saying, early on in my journey especially, was "You can't make up this stuff" as synchronicities occurred to each of us. As we open and believe, stepping forward in our truth, these moments of magic will arrive in our lives more frequently. And sometimes it is simply hard to comprehend. Having friends whom we can call or to whom we can send a text is nice, fun, and reassuring on this journey.

In this chapter about discovering Our Tribe, we will discuss finding Acquaintances Already Connected on their journey, about Finding Our

Tribe, and lastly about the power of Alternative Tribes—of being a tribe of one on occasion, along with discovering our spiritual tribe.

My hope for you on this journey is for you to find your tribe and experience the intimacies that can come with that. There is much we can learn from others on this path. Being part of a like-minded group opens the flow of learning, sharing, and excitement. That said, you may need to go your road alone at times, and that is okay too. This journey is about discovering the balance that works well for you.

Acquaintances Already Connected

We discussed this point briefly earlier in the book. As we embark on this new journey, we may feel a bit uncomfortable in participating in new experiences—of putting ourselves out there into this newfound world. What better way to taste test the world than finding ourselves a sidekick? I know for me, a sidekick who had already experienced whatever it was we were going to do, was even better. Having an experienced sidekick allowed me to ask clarifying questions to help ease any angst. Thank goodness others have already ventured onto this new path before us.

It is interesting, at least here in New England, the closeted world that exists around a raised consciousness. People worry others will judge and think of them as a little crazy, so we often closet this new aspect of us. I am still this way—although I am slowly beginning to share with the world my "crazy." And that's it, right? By calling it crazy, we can diffuse anyone else from judging it as crazy. But it is not crazy. Well, maybe crazy, as in unbelievable! It is amazing, and it is the direction our world is finally going. I digress—back on track. What is interesting is that, as we venture down this road, we discover who else is on this path—and perhaps still closeted a bit as well. We begin to find the people who understand this road we are on, and we can share with them and they with us. It is great to find our network of people, which then allows us to expand the circle and find those people with whom we most connect.

As in business, it's about networking. We talked about my introduction to this new world with my sister and her friend in the very beginning. Between the two of them, they have introduced me to two psychics, the holistic shop, yoga nidra, Reiki, Akashic Records, Access Bars, the shaman, new and full moon ceremonies, a tarot card reader, a polarity practitioner, my chiropractor, a bit of astrology, intuitive healing, and a magical crystal shop. Right! From some of those experiences, I have gone on to meet additional individuals and have other experiences. Find your openings to gain access for yourself. Find those individuals who can introduce you to new experiences.

As we discussed in the Believing chapter, we need to stay true to what we feel in our gut. We should go out there and discover this world, and the people already on the path, but stay true to ourselves. It may feel fine to simply join someone else's journey, and that is okay in the beginning as we are learning what works or does not work for us. We must remember that we will evolve, and we will discover what feels right for our journey. None of us are supposed to be on the exact same journey. We each have a path that we need to develop in discovering our truest self. Our good friends or tribe members can be our anchors, but we need to venture off to explore what we need to learn.

Finding Our Tribe

The experiences we begin to have will open the door for our tribe to develop. Like typical friend circles, our tribe will evolve as we do, and with that, we may find we have a little less in common with other friends in our life if they are not on a similar path. It does not mean we are kicking them to the curb for good, it just means we are giving ourselves the space to explore this new world. Some friends and acquaintances may look at us a little strangely as we describe our new experiences. That is fine. It just means they are not ready themselves, but it should not deter us from exploring what we are feeling pulled toward. Some may not pass judgment but may indicate it is something they are not interested in pursuing themselves. Again, that is fine. And then, there could be friends who join us on this journey, and our friendship is brought to a new level. It comes down to listening to ourselves. Doing what is right for ourselves. Surrounding ourselves with people who support us for who we are. Some of us may choose to live a dual existence in the beginning, and that is fine as well. We will figure it out.

Early on my journey, my tribe began forming around my sister and her friend bringing together a group of women for the new and full moon ceremonies. Each month the group may have looked a little different from the last, depending upon who was available to come from the larger overall group of participants. Some of the women had obviously been on the journey longer and were well into the ease of their practices. And then there were novices like me who, let us be honest, were not completely at ease with any practices nor likely in forming new practices in the presence of strangers. But then the ceremonies progress and we feel the love of the group, we do not sense judgment that may exist in mainstream groups, and there is something freeing about stepping into this new world. It is about positivity, healing, releasing, and setting intentions. The majority of these women are not part of my inner tribe, yet I feel comfortable and have a bond with them. I know they are in the midst of their own self-discovery.

We do form our personal inner circles as well. It is simply human nature to feel a connection to certain individuals. For me, my inner circle or personal tribe is made up of two or three women from the larger tribe, and the rest are people who have been brought into my life separately from that group. It feels like our souls need different individuals in our lives to help us step forward. I sense when I need time with a specific person—male or female. Although my personal tribe may not all gather as a whole, they are still all my personal tribe.

As individuals continue to evolve and rise, their paths may go in different directions. This is fine too. In mainstream life, people get their panties in a bunch when friends leave the nest; however, it is of no issue in this world. There is an understanding that we each are discovering ourselves and may be pulled to what calls to us individually. For example, many from the larger women's group were active in kundalini a while back and attending classes together. Personally, I did not feel a pull toward kundalini and did not participate. And that was fine. As with this whole journey, everyone is evolving, and life is fluid.

Finding our tribe can allow us to have a team with us on this journey. As I mentioned earlier, even if it is simply for the moments of having someone to call to say, "You won't believe what just happened!" or "I just saw an eagle, what do you think that means?" It is an exciting time, and many magical synchronicities are bound to occur that not everyone is ready to hear. It is nice to have the ear of someone who thinks what you are sharing is absolutely fascinating—some may say who "buys into our crazy." We can feel a pull toward this tribe at times too. If it has been a while since we all have gotten together, many of us will feel that need. Coming together is often a grounding experience that can reboot our energies.

Tribe Alternatives

Tribes have so many benefits for us. They give us companionship, reassurance, and offer us introductions to new experiences within this "unconventional" world. I wholeheartedly recommend you find at least one person to embark on this adventure with you, and then maybe the number will grow as you meet others and proceed on your journey.

Now I want to introduce you to variations of the tribe. Although I just finished sharing with you a few of my tribe experiences, I can tell you I have often walked the road by myself. Instead of participating in some of the larger tribe experiences for a period, I tended to be more of a solo kind of person. For me, holding ceremony by myself allowed me to open myself up more, without my own insecurities getting in the way. I was able to practice the routine of a ritual since it was just me. I began some fairly crazy journeying that I needed to do on my own. As things began to open for me, I was guided to keep my journey to myself and allow it to grow—so I did. For two to three months during some fairly intense happenings, I kept mum. Although I eventually shared with a few individuals the events that had transpired, I also began to realize those events were just as magical kept to myself. All in all, I found a healthy combination of group activities and my own personal space was right for me.

This leads me to our guides—our spiritual tribe. I know. Once again, I would not have believed it either. After two years of strolling along on this journey, the last year of the two involving work with the shaman, I still struggled with my intuition. My brain simply got in the way. And then, it began. It was not a simple flip of a light switch. It was a guided sequence of events over time that led to the event that triggered the light being turned on. It was opening, it was the crystals, the meditations, and the clearings that prepared me to receive. And once I began sensing the presence of ancestors and guides, I was hooked. I meditated or journeyed every day. I "talked" to them using my pendulum at the time, mostly because I was still leery of my intuition. "They" became my spiritual tribe. I was spending more time with my spiritual guides than with my physical tribe. It was incredible, but I also learned a few things. First, only offer yourself up to what is in your highest good. Second, ask for protection against unwanted energies. And third, if you play in the spirit world, play more in the physical world. You should not reside too much in the spiritual realm. You must have balance.

With that rush of magic mostly behind me, I went back to the occasional new or full moon ceremony, but it was different now. It was as if I had been given a spiritual confidence boost. It was my own little rocket to surge me forward onto my journey. I now attend ceremonies when I am able or when they fit my schedule with the kids, and this works for my journey.

As with all of this, we jump around. Know there is no right or wrong. Listen to those moments where you may feel the need to explore more on your own for whatever reason. It does not mean you are leaving your tribe; it means you need time to go within to discover more of yourself on your own.

Exercises

1) Find your acquaintance or two. Hopefully, you have already discovered a person with whom you connect. Know this person is not your every-

thing because you will both be exploring your own paths, but consider them your base camp, of sorts. Your journey will evolve quickly and having a sounding board, someone with whom to share stories, book recommendations, new finds, and experiences is awesome.

2) This may push your comfort zone a bit but find a local group to participate in some new experiences with like-minded individuals. If you are having trouble finding a starting place, ask around at your local metaphysical shop. You can sign up for a class at the shop or even through a community program that can introduce you to others beginning this journey. Eventually, you may meet a person with whom you connect, and that may lead to additional opportunities. It is about networking!

3) We have talked about meditations, crystal grid making, self-reflection, and a few other activities that we do in solitude. Gift yourself the time and space to explore these things on your own. Begin with creating your daily ritual, and then explore from there. You will feel the pull toward what you need to do next on your journey.

My advice to you is to allow your tribe to form organically. As with this whole journey, we evolve and need to remain fluid with our expectations as we walk our path. As we find our tribe, know that our personal tribe is our spiritual family, and they will be there for us as we progress on our journey and we for them. We will individually form our inner circle or personal tribe with people who will be different from others within our base tribe. Likely, there will be overlap, but we will find the people on this journey to whom we most connect. There will also be spiritual acquaintances as we each traverse different areas of this spiritual journey. When we feel the draw to a particular practice, we can connect with that person. Once again, similar to business. We have our subject matter experts whom we can call to discuss a more specific topic. Finally, we will likely discover our own spiritual tribe and guides in time. Our spiritual guides provide us with wisdom and will allow us to grow even more. Through our journey, we each will discover the healthy combination that defines our personal tribe.

Chapter Ten

Creativity

Although the Cambridge Dictionary does define creativity as "the ability to produce or use original and unusual ideas," searching for a definition of creativity outside of "to be creative" took me down a rabbit hole for a bit.

When I emerged from the rabbit hole, I realized we have already discussed through this book many of the ingredients for developing our own creativity—for creativity is defined by each of us. It is as unique as we are and as this journey is for us individually. Creativity is the delicious cake from our personal creative oven—the product of our ingredients. Think of what we placed or are placing into our canoe. We are placing knowledge, experiences, interests, hobbies, desires, dreams, opinions, and all that we are into our canoe—the ingredients. These ingredients mixed with gratitude for all our moments, being in the present, attuning to our senses, getting out in nature, and everything else we have discussed creates our individual cake of creativity.

Our unique assembly of ingredients explains why artists and all of us can have such vastly different interpretations in our creations.

Although many of us may believe we are not inherently creative, contrary to this, it seems we are all naturally creative. It seems our creativity has been taught out of us over time, but do not fret. There appears to be hope for us left-brainers to reintroduce creativity back into our lives, beginning with the handful of ingredients we already have in our cupboards. Yes, even we left-brained linear thinkers have likely already assembled our creative cupboard with a few ingredients, even if we did not realize it—and we may be unknowingly using them now within our careers.

What it takes for our creativity to flourish is time and practice, like anything. Some of our greatest creative artists had their gifts nourished early, and then they practiced and honed their crafts for hours, days, years. Think of how elite athletes prepare for their sports; it's the same concept. Our dedication may be to a lesser degree, but we can still apply ourselves enough to get our creative juices flowing, especially once we fill our cupboards with even more creative ingredients.

Although we are going to dive into creativity outside of the workplace in this chapter, it is fascinating to witness industry recognizing the need for creative minds within the workforce. And it makes sense. The competition to be the best does not allow for status quo. Businesses must put on their creative caps to find the next best thing to keep them at the forefront of their respective industries.

So what does this mean for us linear-minded individuals who may not consider ourselves creative? We may be able to understand that offering creative solutions within our jobs may allow us to flourish, but why do we need to incorporate creativity into our daily lives outside of work if it is simply not our "thing"? Well, my rational thinkers, there are many benefits of unleashing our creativity, which we will get into further in the chapter. These benefits will allow us to step into the truest version of ourselves, believe it or not. It is time for all of us to replenish our arts and crafts supplies, tap into our growing number of creative ingredients, and begin creating!

Over the last five years on this journey, I have dabbled in a few creative endeavors. My kids are now teenagers and are not as much into arts and crafts any longer so unless I can reign in the tribe or convince my kids to partake, I am a solo creator. As I write this, I am having my biggest pull toward creativity. Now, considering I have not produced multiple pieces of any artwork of any particular type, for the most part, I am going to go out on a limb here. I may have to delete this paragraph at a later time if I do not follow through. Here is my *aha!* moment as I write this book. Since I was young, I have been drawn to Claude Monet and impressionism, but I have never attempted to paint in this way. On two volunteering field trips to the Museum of Fine Arts, Boston with my kids' classes in the last handful of years, I found myself in the Monet exhibit trying to get ten- and eleven-year-olds to appreciate the paintings. I felt a connection that I did not feel in the other exhibits. In November, a person on social media mentioned it was Monet's birthday and there it was! I needed to interpret a few ideas in my brain into impressionistic paintings. So the last two nights I have watched videos on "how to." Although I have no artistic education or real interest in painting, I feel the need to do this. What I find interesting is I now realize the paintings to which I have always been drawn are either impressionistic or abstract. I think I have finally resigned myself to the fact I find comfort in the perfect imperfection of these types of art. If you are reading this paragraph, it means I followed through with this challenge for myself.

So we listen. We listen to what speaks to us. We create what feels like something we should be creating in that moment. One of my first creations on this journey was whittling a replication of a little clog originally whittled by my grandfather, who passed when my mother was eighteen. That was my only whittling creation. We listen.

My hope for you on this journey is if you are not already tapping into your creativity, for you to step outside of your comfort zone. Give yourself permission to have fun and release any judgment of yourself or any creations you bring to light.

In this chapter on Creativity, we will discuss the Source and Benefits of Creativity; a sampling of the various Types of Creative Modes available to us; and Developing our Creativity.

As you read this chapter, I hope you will become inspired to open your creative portal. Know that I am right there with you. Keep hopping back on the creative rail to realize all the benefits it offers. You are already assembling your creative ingredients as you walk your path. These ingredients will allow you to create in your unique way.

The Source and Benefits of Creativity

Creativity comes from deep within us. To be specific it resides in our second chakra, our sacral chakra. This is home to our creativity and reproduction, and with it, the seat of pleasure. Take the seat of pleasure and all its indulgences, along with the home of reproduction, and we have the potential for blocked energy due to incidents from this or previous lives within that space. I can personally speak to this one. One intuitive practitioner told me she saw a dagger stuck in my sacral chakra. Another intuitive healer told me she saw my sacral chakra as black. Whether or not my blackened, wounded sacral chakra had anything to do with my uncreative self, one can only presume. So I did what any self-awakening person on this journey would do, I worked on clearing my sacral chakra.

Whether someone sees black in our sacral chakra or not, it would be a good idea to clear the energy as we work on unleashing our creativity. Remember, we begin with the root chakra and move our way up to the crown to allow an unobstructed flow of life force energy through our bodies. If our sacral chakra is mucked up, our energy is not getting very far. Think of a big colander inside our body, our vessel. As life's complications happen and we begin this journey, our colander may not have many holes to allow our life force energy to flow. As we begin to heal, open, and live more presently, more holes begin to appear in the colander, or the holes get larger allowing more energy to flow through. Every time we push ourselves beyond limits set for ourselves physically, emotionally, spiritually, intellectually, socially, or creatively we increase the size of these holes and add more. Think about how we feel when we accomplish something outside our comfort zone. It is exhilarating. A surge of energy. Eventually, maybe the colander is one big hole, allowing a forceful stream of life force energy running through our bodies.

Let us first work on clearing those energy centers. Crystals are a great way to work with clearing our chakras, as we have previously discussed. Our sacral chakra is orange, which makes cornelian, amber, and citrine great to use. There are additional stones or crystals that would also be appropriate. Find what calls to you. Breathwork is another great exercise in moving the stuck energy, as is scheduling time with a Reiki practitioner, an energy worker. And lastly, step outside your comfort zone and simply create!

Bringing creativity into our lives likely brings more benefits than we realize. Many of these will carry over into our everyday life and assist us on our path of self-healing. As Picasso said, "*The purpose of art is washing the dust of daily life off our souls.*"

And, creating is that, right? We can stop our daily life for a moment of time and simply create. Allowing ourselves to be in the present while creating brings an awareness to the things we are doing in that moment. Here is a great opportunity to practice the skill of being in the present. Allow ourselves to immerse our senses and our state of being in creating a piece of artwork, whatever it may be. At times, this way of creating can be meditative in nature. It becomes not about simply getting the project done to check off our to-do list for the day but feeling part of ourselves within this new creation.

Creating is about releasing our insecurities. Ultimately, there is no right or wrong way to create. Some of us may need practice with this. *It does not matter* what other people think about what we are creating or have created. Art is an expression of ourselves. It is fine if we are not professionally trained in a technique. If we feel the need to improve, we can research and practice. In the end, we are creating what we feel, not what we think, meaning each of us should have different interpretations within our creations.

Creating is an amazing way to work with building our intuition and it can begin simply with "What should I draw...paint...sew...felt... sculpt...sing...bake?" Often this can bring in building our confidence as well. With each stroke, line, or stitch, we are faced with a decision to make. We learn to trust. Trust ourselves and trust our intuition. Develop our confidence not just in this artwork, but in stepping forward with confidence on this journey and in life.

Creating helps us get in touch with our intuition, our thoughts, our feelings, and, perhaps, our state of mind in a given moment—including stress. Creating can be therapeutic in processing our emotions. In a sense, it can be our own form of self-counseling. Look at the trend of art and play therapy these days. As my kids dealt with processing the divorce, they saw counselors who used art and play as part of their sessions. This was extremely therapeutic for one of my children. At the time, I was blown away at how much it helped process feelings and emotions.

As always, when we begin to attempt to bring creativity into our lives, we need to be kind to ourselves. Not only from a judgment standpoint, but in finding consistency with it. I will find a creative hour or two, and then not find another for days, weeks, or even months. That is okay. If I look back over the past year, I know I have been more creative during this year than the last—so I am stepping forward.

Creating can help us process the healing needed within the old us, while also discovering this new version of ourselves who we are...creating as well.

Types of Creativity

Art categories seem as varied as the interpretations of each one. Although there are defined categories of art, I feel we each have the ability to create whatever we want to create and call it art.

Years ago, the kids and I went to the Museum of Modern Art in New York City. In one room, all by itself, were thousands of small silver-wrapped mints (we assumed) in a perfect square on the floor—in an area, I am going to guesstimate, was twelve feet square. That was art. In its own room. In a major museum. In such instances, I always wonder about the discussions around including a piece I do not fully understand in an exhibit. More to the point is whatever qualifies as art is up to our individual interpretation—and sometimes that of a curator.

Finding what type or category of art speaks to us individually will come. Personally, I am still discovering what brings me joy when I attempt to be creative as opposed to feeling like a fish out of water, but I keep plugging along. Like everything, try something out before passing judgment on it. You just never know.

Painting with acrylics may be the easy go-to for some of us novices. In fact, around many cities, there are group painting events (often with drinks), which make an easy test drive for us before we go purchase our own set of everything. My partner and I did this for a date night a few years ago. He then purchased paint, brushes, and easels for us to host a paint night at our house—which then became a paint and poker night. We have hosted such nights three or four times since, and interestingly, I don't believe he has painted at any of them. A little self-serving for a poker night, perhaps—I say with a smile. Anyway, this was a great introduction for me. Going forward, it seems time for us to branch off and paint what speaks to us individually instead of using a common tutorial. A post-pandemic party, for sure.

Watercolors are another nice and simple entry into playing around to see what speaks to us. And within each of these painting categories are different techniques. There are so many options for us out there, and the internet is a plethora of information and tutorials to get us started.

Using fibers is an additional category for those of us new to the creative path. My mother taught me to knit a couple of years ago. I knitted one piece. Strips that I then sewed together to make a mat for ceremony. Was it pretty? Nope. I have a new appreciation for people who can knit or crochet. For me, I think my mind would explode. For you, maybe it would be the perfect form of creativity or stress relief.

I was also introduced to felting with wool. This felting thing is a little more my speed. To begin, a group of us tried out needle felting. I used one of those kits you can purchase online to make a cute little owl and my kids made creatures as well. This is an easy entry into a creative attempt, and a fun little family project if you are looking for such a project as well.

And then I was introduced to wet felting and a little light went off. The first thing I made was a medicine bag. I loved it but felt like it belonged to someone else, so I gave it away. Then I saw a vision of a mat for ceremony that I was to give away as well. I made a practice one for myself and about nine months later, I just made the other mat and gifted it to that person. I recently completed another vision I had almost a year ago. I am going to go out on a limb and say, for the time being, felting may be where my creative time will be spent. The simple fact I am having visions about it makes me listen a little more closely.

As with everything, we need to listen to our gut, our intuition. Give different modes a try to see what speaks to us. Or maybe it will only speak to us for a mere moment for a particular purpose. Like digging out the sewing machine after a decade to make pandemic masks for the family. A couple of years ago, I was briefly drawn to string art. It was a yin-yang sign I saw while poking around online. My partner prepped a board for me, and with no pattern, I figured out how many nails would be needed, measured out all seventy-two of them, and hammered away. I made the symbol with green and blue string. It looks like earth. It sits on my bookshelf and reminds me to keep balance. My partner prepped a second board for me, and I have never used it. I feel like I was only meant to make that one piece.

Whatever the creative endeavor or type of art, we should allow ourselves the space to see where it takes us. It could be pottery, painting ceramics, sculpting, writing, singing, playing music, painting, photography, calligraphy, carving, felting, knitting, crocheting, cooking, upcycling, sewing, embroidering, weaving, baking, and anything else that *"dusts off our souls."*

Developing Our Creativity

"All children are artists. The problem is how to remain an artist once he grows up."

—Pablo Picasso

As left-brained thinkers, many of us have closed off the creative side of being. I say "closed off" because at some point in our lives it existed. Now, knowing we have developed or are developing the creative ingredients through this journey, we simply need to wake up our creativity. To do that, we may need to chip off some of the reasons why we do not create. Here is my biggest reason: what I envision creating and my expectations of what I create are never fulfilled by the reality of my creation. A little case of perfectionism, maybe? The way I have always dealt with this issue, in all aspects of life, is to simply not do it. If we never do "it," then we cannot fail. Problem solved. Okay, not a healthy solution. How about another reason? There are more productive things that should be done in this moment. I am hopeful the younger generations will begin to lose this mindset, but we must teach them the balance of life—and first, we must embody it for ourselves.

Some of us will need to take the first step of removing the pressure around being creative, and this begins with allotting time to be creative. To be in the present with being creative. Removing all other distractions. With that done, now we can work on having fun with our creativity. There is no need for there to be pressure to create, to create something "perfect." By allowing our creativity the space in time and allowing our beings to be free to have fun with what we are creating, happiness will ensue. How nice does that moment of time sound?

Developing our creativity can take on as many forms as the type of art with which we decide to create. Opening our senses is always a good step as it brings an awareness, an aliveness to life. Of course, getting out in nature is both revitalizing for all the reasons we have already discussed, as well as for inspiration for our work of art.

I am going to digress on this nature piece for a second. The impressionistic movement was around a new, more casual way of painting, along with using the brighter colors discovered in nature. Look at Monet's paintings. He was able to move his "studio" outside to embrace what nature offered him, including the fleeting changes of light. This painting technique and these colors were not the norm of the time and were snubbed by the critics accustomed to the darker more academic paintings of that period. Nature inspires creativity.

Going to art museums, reading art books, or simply going online and falling down various rabbit holes can inspire you to create. In fact, online is where I found the yin-yang string art. I felt a draw to find something I could create. Something that did not feel beyond my abilities and so I went online, and there it was. I knew I needed to make it.

And finally for the big one. Allow ourselves to fail. Yes, I know. This is a hard pill to swallow for so many of us. Not all our artwork will be a masterpiece, and that is okay. Most of us are not professionally trained artists, nor will we likely invest the time to become one. We need to release our expectations that we will want to wear the sweater, hang the painting, or sing in public. Instead, look to each moment for the entertainment value it provides, the lessons we learn, and the enjoyment we have while creating. We have all heard the adage that it is when we fail that we grow the most. Accept our creative failures and maybe even laugh when they occur.

Exercises

1) Although you may be working on clearing all your chakras, let us give focus to your sacral chakra to allow you to kick-start your creativity. It may take some time to fully clear it, yet you can begin. Gather stones and crystals that resonate with the sacral chakra—a quick few are carnelian, amber, citrine, and tiger's eye. Carry one or more of these in your pockets, place them in a dish beside your workstation, or use them in a clearing meditation. When using them in a clearing meditation, try to incorporate breathwork as well. If time and money permit, find a Reiki practitioner (ask around for a referral if possible) to help you move any stuck energy. The act of creating will aid in clearing your sacral chakra too.

2) Time to get inspired. Let yourself go down some rabbit holes. Look at books, go online, visit Pinterest, or head to a museum. Discover what inspires you. You are not necessarily looking to replicate a particular piece, but to discover your interpretation of the artwork that inspires you. Of course, a great place for inspiration is to step out into nature as well.

3) Schedule yourself creative time. Maybe begin on a weekend morning. This is not multitasking time. No unloading the dishwasher in between brush strokes. Allow yourself to just be in the moment. Be in the present. Create whatever you feel like creating in that moment and without judgment. Simply have fun discovering a little of yourself.

As you begin your creative practice or continue an existing practice, here is something for you to keep in mind. You may produce a piece of artwork embodying the emotions you needed to release in that moment. It is a personal piece. Yet, you are not the only one in this world who may feel those emotions. There may be others, not everyone, who can also relate to those emotions when they see or hear your work of art. They may have an immediate appreciation for your work of art. That is the power of creating. Not that all of us will put our works of art out into the world; likely most of us will keep them within our own walls. But be aware of the positive impact that any one of us could have by simply sharing the power of our creativity.

My advice to you in this chapter on Creativity is to make time in your week to begin exercising your creative abilities. Push yourself outside of your comfort zone by attempting a new mode of art. Maybe you only produce one piece, and that is fine. Just allow yourself to enjoy the experience and to reap the benefits of being creative. The fact that all of us can produce a work of art is inspiring. We feel a sense of pride in ourselves when we can see, hear, smell, touch, or taste a tangible product of our making. Embrace this. It is the life force energy flowing.

Chapter Eleven

Spiritual Toolbox

When I picture a spiritual toolbox, I picture a little cartoon character walking around with his red toolbox, and then rummaging around to find the tool that fits perfectly for a given situation. This is going to be us!

Why do we need a spiritual toolbox? For many of us, the toolbox simply offers us new ways of approaching and addressing our life experiences. We are evolving and acquiring new tools to live a more fulfilled life. How we handle certain situations will change—for the better. For some of us, the toolbox offers us tools we can use to help others move forward on their journey in whatever form that may take.

What goes into our spiritual toolbox is up to each of us. There will be times when there will be a strong pull for an item to be placed in our toolbox. Other times we may not fully know why we put an item in our toolbox, but eventually, we will see its purpose when the time is right. So what types of things go into our toolbox? Knowledge, traits, intuition, experiences, certifications, and licenses are a few items able to find their way into our toolbox. And, in the end, our toolbox will be personalized for our individual journey.

Early in the book, we discussed the fact that we will each feel the pull toward what calls to us. And, for the most part, no one person's journey will be the same as another. Nor should it be. We are all little snowflakes and should be different from the snowflake next to us. We can venture down a similar road as another—for having a partner on this journey is fun—but know you will and should be directed toward your own tools as well. At the end of the day, we are all evolving to our purpose. A calling that will also evolve over time. But the common thread is raising the universal consciousness. And that thread can be in healing our own being, which creates a light to raise up others. The thread can be helping to heal others so they also can become a light to raise up others. The thread can be becoming a source whom others can turn to through our message of speech, education, art, writing, song, or other means to help raise up the general population—to inspire them to become a light.

As I always do, here I must remind us not to judge our toolbox against the toolbox of another. For a while, we may not understand what we should even put in our toolbox. And being, perhaps, a little competitive, we may get frustrated with our seemingly empty toolbox. Especially as we watch others fill up their toolboxes. All I can tell you is to be patient and be kind to yourself. Sometimes we may not even realize our toolbox is filling. Keep in mind the hare and the tortoise. We all get to where we are supposed to be. It just may take some of us a bit longer. We must trust what the Universe has in store for us and keep working on ourselves in the meantime.

Take me, for example. I began as not only a skeptic but simply an unconscious individual. I was so wrapped up in my own little world and daily living or surviving, I did not open myself to self-discovery. As a result, it took some time to unwrap that package and begin pulling back the layers. To open myself to believing in something more. There was a lot of healing to do first. Even though I wanted to *catch up* with others, focusing on my own inner healing was a necessity before I could do anything for the greater good. Even now, I simply take it day by day. In fact, as I am writing this book, I have begun receiving messages from a guide. I know. I know. I will explain more in the final chapter. Anyway, just yesterday I was asking my typical barrage of questions when I got this: *It is inside you. This knowledge you seek. There is no need to ask it. It is there for you. Give it a chance to be heard.* And so this is my message for you as well. The knowledge of our path is within all of us, we just need to trust and listen.

As we move into the rest of the Spiritual Toolbox chapter, we will discuss the items we can place in our toolbox. Specifically, we will get into our Intuition, various Certifications and Licenses, and lastly our Experiences and all the benefits they bring with them.

My hope for you in this chapter is for you to fully understand how transformational this journey is for all of us. It is exciting to consider how we are creating a better version of ourselves that is unique to us individually. Our journey is our journey; however, the potential impact our ripple effect can have on the world is far-reaching. Our toolbox will never be empty. As soon as we took our first step onto this path, we began to place items in our toolbox. Even if the first item is a simple awareness. An awareness of a better version of ourselves waiting, and we are ready to begin the journey toward it.

Intuition

Here we sit. This intuition thing, am I right? Okay, we all have those moments of feeling something is not quite right. This is our intuition. So we have it. But what about those people who see things, hear things, sense things…they know things! We do not have that kind of intuition—in this moment or to that level. I am guessing this is the way most of us feel. Yet, we all want intuition in our toolbox. We all need intuition in our toolbox. How do we get there?

As I began my journey, there was me, and then there were others who had likely been developing their intuition to some degree their entire lives. As a result, beginning the journey for them was like jumping on a treadmill already moving, whereas I was like the first car we drove as teenagers that often would not start, so we would hold the ignition attempting to "turn it over." I am going to say, for me at least, this has been one of my larger points of frustration on the journey.

I can tell you we need to be patient. We need to trust—both the Universe and our own intuition. Flip off the switch to our logical minds and let our intuition develop. And, I know, easier said than done, unfortunately. I get it. If you are like me, we get our thinking brain involved, and it becomes the awkward teenager stepping all over the progress we have made toward developing our intuition. In those moments where I do get my intuition working, I get so excited and I react to that excitement; this brings along my thinking brain, and my intuition runs for cover.

So how do we develop our intuition? For some of us, there is already enough of an inkling; we need only develop it by learning to trust it and practice. For many of us, however, it may take a little more work. Early in my journey, I purchased a pendulum. It was like training wheels for me. It took the pressure off and limited my own reactions because it felt like someone else was telling me these things. I began with basic *yes* and *no* questions and eventually used it with an alphabet grid, as I mentioned previously. I became addicted to it. I kept the pendulum in my pocket at all times. Eventually, the shaman informed me I needed to begin to trust my intuition and stop relying on the pendulum—for the intuition was inside of me. He told me to look to my intuition, and if I felt like I *needed* validation, then use the pendulum for that purpose. On the way home immediately after the session with him, I stopped at the grocery store and dropped the pendulum in the parking lot as I was getting out of the car. I did not notice until I got home. Without time to go back, and a snowstorm coming in, I was unable to return until three days later. I found the pendulum in the plowed snow of the parking lot (yes, as desperate as it sounds) and the chain was broken off. I said to myself, "It's a sign." But I could not exist without the pendulum, so I went and purchased a new chain and attached it. I immediately dropped the pendulum on the tiled bathroom floor, and it shattered. Another sign! Do I have one today? Yes, but I eventually weaned myself off completely… almost. And here is a little secret about the pendulum. There is no little spirit inside of it making it move. It is our intuition. Gasp! If you go this route, have an awareness of these facts I share with you so you may avoid my little pitfalls…but it is fun!

Honestly, if we keep stepping forward with everything we have talked about in this book, our intuition is going to come alive. Attuning to our senses in nature is an extraordinary way to work with our intuition or simply being out in nature more. Meditation is a fantastic way as well. I know it was for me. This is where I began to sense things occurring.

For a long time, meditation was the only space where I sensed things… and then I would confirm with my pendulum. What recently began to occur for me is that I sense words mostly when I have a wooden pencil and paper in hand, and then magic occurs. We are all different and are quirky little creatures. Your intuition will arrive when it is supposed to arrive, but you can work with it too.

Now, back to the toolbox. In adding our growing and evolving intuition to our toolbox, a whole new world of opportunities opens to us. It adds magic to our abilities as we journey down this road. My sister's Reiki sessions became intuitive healing sessions. My massage therapist can sense the areas of the body that need more attention. The other massage and polarity therapist I have seen will discuss with you what she has picked up on after a session. The shaman is an artist and intuitively creates. An acquaintance who is a tattoo artist is also a Reiki practitioner who intuitively helps her clients create their tattoos. Another friend is a teacher, and as soon as she took her first step onto this path, intuition flooded her. Intuitive abilities change the playing field. Intuition is the cherry on top of the sundae of life.

Certifications and Licenses

Whether for our own use or to be used with others, acquiring certifications and licenses may feel like a natural step on our path. Whether or not we use them immediately will be determined. Whether they are used for our own purpose along our path or for the greater good will be determined as well. Time will tell.

By certifications, I am referring to such modalities as Reiki, polarity, craniosacral therapy, Akashic Records, Access Bars, yoga, and restorative yoga to name a few. As far as licenses, I am referring to massage therapy, acupuncture, aesthetics, and the like. We could even throw in areas of specialty such as astrology, tarot reading, and mediumship.

I have mentioned my sister as an example a few times in this book. She initially began acquiring her certifications at warp speed. With her she-shed built and her certificates framed, she evolved with her intuition and now combines all her skills, knowledge, and intuition into intuitive healing. When she creates sacred space for a client, she intuitively senses what a person needs, and the session forms around what feels necessary. She pulls from the tools in her spiritual toolbox.

Another highly intuitive friend is an astrology wizard, and it has been her love since she was a teenager. As she journeyed on her path, she acquired various certifications and even became a licensed aesthetician. She opened her own shop and provided the most magical facials, incorporating Reiki and her intuitive touch. With the pandemic, she closed up shop and, having already made a vast number of connections in the magical world, she has focused her energies into her true love of astrology. And just like that, we can now find her on various sites sharing her wisdom and as a frequent guest on other podcasts.

I was introduced to an extraordinary young woman who went to school for psychology and is a licensed clinical social worker. While completing her schooling, beginning a career, and eventually opening her own practice, she became Reiki III certified, received training in intuition and meditation, and is a registered yoga instructor, along with her additional academic certifications. She has melded all this knowledge and experience into creating an integrated holistic healing practice covering mind, body, and spirit for her clients.

People are stepping onto their path and creating a journey unique to them. As I type this, I am sitting here in amazement at what these spectacular people are putting into their toolboxes as they step forward in their purpose. All of us have this ability. I could keep sharing the paths of people who are popping into my mind, but I will stop here. You get the point. There are so many combinations of tools we can assemble to get us where we need to go.

I also want you to know that sometimes it may appear as if we miss the mark when attaining a certification or license if we do not put it to immediate use or truly know why we acquired it in the first place. Just know there was a reason for the acquisition of this new skill. Do not look at it as a misfire. There was likely a reason, although the purpose may not fully unfold until a later time.

For me, I have never had the urge to attain any certifications or licenses except for insurance and real estate. I simply do not feel or sense I am meant to go down this path on my journey. At least not yet. If this is you or becomes you, try to be at ease with it. We are all different. I know I keep repeating that point, but sometimes we need to be reminded. For some of us, our toolbox will look vastly different from those of the people I just mentioned. It has taken me a few years to find peace with this.

Begin to discover if you are meant to include certifications or licenses in your spiritual toolbox. If these practices do not feel compatible with your path currently, let them go for now. If these modalities have sparked a bit of intrigue, have an experience with one or more of them to have a closer look. Talk to current practitioners, ask questions, and then proceed at your own pace.

Experiences

This is the place where we left-brained, rational-minded people may find many of our tools for our spiritual toolbox. Let us see it, touch it, and absorb it. I am talking about experiences fueled by having time with them, applying the knowledge that we have gathered, and in the act of creating. Creating—yes, creating. Although we just finished talking about our potential struggle with creativity in the last chapter, creating can represent the tangible. And we know that people like us can wrap our minds around tangible a bit more easily than the intangible.

The gathering of experiences through hands-on practice, knowledge, and creativity are tools. Once again, we may not fully realize their place on our path until a later time, but the reason will arrive. We have discussed most of these items in other chapters already, but we will address them again here with the twist of how they become tools in our toolbox.

Absorbing knowledge through books, documentaries, videos, or podcasts can build a foundation of information and understanding to this whole journey. What is interesting is as we read books from various people coming from various places, both figuratively and literally, there can be a thread of commonality in the stories. There is a universal thread weaving through time and place. It is an astonishing fact with so many books of this spiritual journey. The knowledge we absorb provides us with insights and perspectives that we can then apply to our experiences.

Through this journey, I have become a book junkie. Most fascinating to me is how and when these books arrive, along with when I feel the pull to select them from my bookshelf for the first or second or third time. Whenever this happens, there appears to be a reason for it. At this point, I simply smile. I understand these books have prepared me to write and have solidified my knowledge of this new world I am journeying within. Writing was nowhere near my radar when I began.

Experiences come in many forms. Experiences bring life to the knowledge we have acquired. Experiences to further our intuition. Experiences to learn more about various spiritual modalities to see if they speak to us. Experiences to feed our creativity, which in turn helps to fuel our intuition. Immersing ourselves in experiences helps us to determine what feels right to place in our toolbox. What does not fit, we let slip away. Yet we retain the awareness from that experience.

I have received Reiki or polarity from a few practitioners, had Akashic Record and Access Bars sessions, and received various forms of bodywork. Based on these sessions, I know these practices and my being are not meant to synchronize. I love receiving them, but the thought of acquiring the skills and offering the services is not "my thing." I have recognized this (without needing to go the road of certification or licensing) and let them slip away.

Having the experience of creating may not seem like a toolbox-worthy tool, especially for those of us who may struggle in this realm. However, creativity is a broad category. And, like everything on this journey, we simply may not know how it will eventually meander its way onto our path. Perhaps our art is meant only for ourselves, but just maybe it is meant to be received by another.

As we discussed in the Creativity chapter, we can be talking about a laundry list of creative categories: pottery, painting ceramics, sculpting, writing, singing, playing music, painting, photography, calligraphy, carving, felting, knitting, crocheting, cooking, upcycling, sewing, embroidering, weaving, baking, and anything thing else you wish to add.

If we find a pull toward any of these items or multiple items, we should have an experience with them. It can be a pleasant surprise to see how creating can weave its way into our storylines. Writing has entered my toolbox, somewhat unexpectedly. My sister has begun selling some of her felted art projects. The shaman is an artist who sells his art creations at shows. Another acquaintance evolved her love of plants and herbs to making teas and herbal remedies. My partner's sister writes songs and is compiling her songs for release. My teenage daughter has created note cards from her photos and has begun selling them and donating a portion of the proceeds to a charity she supports. My mother spends the winters knitting hats and mittens to give away to friends, family, people in need, and Special Olympians. We all have a creative gift (or two or three) within us ready for a place in our toolbox. Time will tell how and when we put them into play.

Exercises

1) Use meditation to begin practicing with your intuition. Sit in meditation with an intention, such as working with a particular chakra. Allow yourself to sense and be aware of the colors or whatever else you see or sense. Attempt not to project images. That part can be difficult because we want to "see" visions. Be patient. If you "feel" the need to use a crystal or reposition your hands, do this. This is your intuition. Do not get frustrated; it will come. In the beginning, five minutes is enough time— or do more if you would like.

2) Plan an experience with a practice such as Reiki, polarity, Akashic Records, Access Bars, or even a tarot, astrology, or mediumship reading. This experience can serve multiple purposes. It can be part of your self-healing and self-care, as well as determining if you feel the pull toward learning more about the practice of that modality. Perhaps it will end up in your spiritual toolbox.

3) Become a sponge of knowledge and experiences. Absorb all that interests you even when you do not fully understand its purpose. Begin with a book that may seem a little outside of where you currently are in your self-discovery. In time, you will think back to that book and realize the connection it has to the many additional pieces of information you have accumulated for your spiritual toolbox. Watch the common thread weave itself through religions, continents, and centuries.

Through this chapter, we addressed the variety of items we can place in our spiritual toolbox from our developing Intuition to Certifications, Licenses, and areas of specialty to the Experiences that solidify our newfound knowledge derived from books, documentaries, videos, and podcasts, as well as through new creative ventures. Taste-test whatever speaks to you. Again, you may not know what, where, why, when, or how a new item will fit into this journey you have embarked upon, but there is likely a reason.

As always, my advice to you is to be kind to yourself and be patient. As I mentioned, the simple act of becoming aware of a better version of you is already a tool in your new spiritual toolbox. The remaining items will be added over time. Do not make it a contest. Life to this point may have been a contest, but this journey is not. Trust yourself, your intuition, and the Universe, and continue to step forward discovering your tools for your spiritual toolbox.

Chapter Twelve

Spirituality

This chapter is a tougher one for me. As I mentioned in an earlier chapter, I was not raised in a religious household. Combine that fact with my linear way of thinking, and I did not see spirituality as a missing entity in my life. If my mother mentioned to me that she was praying for a family member going through a health concern, I would give my obligatory eye roll. As I somewhat matured, my canned response to religion was, "While I appreciate the church's sense of community, I feel my parents raised me with a sound moral structure, and I am not in need of an institution placing its moral code on me as well."

It was not until this journey we are now on that I reconsidered and separated spirituality from religion. As we walk down this journey of awakening, perhaps spiritual awakening, what does spirituality actually mean? How does it differ from religion? Have we, especially we Westerners, created a blend of beliefs to form a mere concept of how we choose to walk our path and labeled our blend as spiritual?

I am certain there can be, has been, and will be great debate on this matter given the passion with which people often express their beliefs. We are not going to necessarily get into all that here. Wars have been fought for many centuries over this. Instead, we will use this chapter to simply separate the two out and realize like everything else on this journey, it is our individual prerogative to believe in whatever speaks to our soul. And, as such, maybe we simply need a little food for thought to process this aspect of the journey we are on.

Although we will get into more specifics of the differences between spirituality and religion in a moment, we can at least define them here. I am going to stick to Merriam-Webster once again. Religion is defined as "a personal set or institutionalized system of religious attitudes, beliefs, and practices" as well as a "commitment or devotion to religious faith or observance."

Finding a definition of spirituality outside of religion was not as easy. The dictionary definitions tended to be more about the "state of being spiritual," although the Oxford Dictionary did define spirituality as, "The quality of being concerned with the human spirit or soul as opposed to material or physical things." Otherwise, it was defined by people on various websites—meaning it was defined by individuals according to their interpretation of spirituality. Perfect!

Perhaps an oversimplified explanation defines religion as a more organized structure with a uniform set of beliefs, laws, codes, or expected conduct established by the religious institution for its followers who have faith in this institution and the higher being they worship. Spirituality, on the other hand, has to do with creating an individual awareness of something greater than self through spiritual seeking. There is no code and there is no right or wrong. There can be worship—or not. The path of seeking can differ for every person, and the path of spirituality is defined by every person for their individual journey. In fact, for some, it is a combination of their learned traditional religious beliefs married with their own spiritual seeking. This is how I interpret religion and spirituality.

Whether through religious faith or inner spirituality, opening ourselves up to believing is a gigantic step for many of us. And, seeking an understanding of life—both our own and universal—is a spiritual experience. When we begin to open ourselves up, we feel the need to know a few of the big answers to life. It does not matter if we are come from a traditional religious background or are on an individual spiritual journey. We are all doing the best we can to discover our path in this lifetime. It is about finding our truth.

As we move further into this chapter on Spirituality, we are going to Dig into Spirituality outside of religion, discuss The Presence we feel that is greater than us, as well as the spirits of The Natural World.

My hope for you is that you will open yourself up to spirituality or spiritual awakening. By this point, you understand I am still on this road with you. We will all have moments where we will believe with all our might…and then a little time will go by, and we will begin to question those feelings that we believed wholeheartedly just a week ago. Our best bet of feeling a constant stream of spirituality is to do our best to remain connected. Connected to our path, to the present, to the feeling of something greater than ourselves, and to the miracles available to us through nature. It is a connection to the universal energy within all of us.

Digging into Spirituality

Love. Gratitude. Compassion. Kindness. Awareness. Being Present.

By applying the above words to most moments in life, those moments have the opportunity to be spiritual. And in bringing this reverence to our every day—that becomes our spirituality.

What I find fascinating in this self-designed spirituality practice is that we evolve, thus creating our own ever-changing, unique path of spiritual awakening.

Maybe this is the draw for many of us. Spirituality feels unrestrained and limitless. We may pull from a religious tradition such as Buddhism or Catholicism; however, we are melding those beliefs into our unique blend of spirituality. In many ways, it is a journey of free-form spiritual self-discovery. If the goal of spirituality is to raise our own level of consciousness and consequently aid in raising the universal consciousness, we will likely feel the pull to step forward on our path with many of the stepping-stones and tools we have discussed in the book; however, which tools resonate for us personally will be an individual decision.

Being the type of person I am (and you may be), this path gives me a sense of controlling my path of spirituality even though I am working on relinquishing control and trusting the Universe. Does that make sense?

I know the path of spirituality is my religion. I define it. I write it in pencil because my definition can evolve. I can research and experience a practice, and then keep it, modify it, or let it slip away. This appeals to my way of being.

What I love about spirituality is that there is a subset of the population on this journey—this journey that differs for most everyone, yet it is all-inclusive. We feel a connection to others finding their way and evolving on their journey. And although our journeys may differ, the universal thread is love, light, kindness, compassion, and gratitude. How amazing is that?

After a handful of years on this journey, I am still in such awe of this *nontraditional* world. In all the craziness of 2020, a connective thread has been weaving together a group of women around me. I feel it with each person to whom I become connected—and they typically feel it as well. The ultimate unified purpose has yet to unfold. Along with my inner tribe, this draw has been to a person I did not know in New York, another in Florida, an old acquaintance now living in New Mexico, and a transplant to Maine. We each feel we have been connected for a reason. Again, our paths are all different, yet the undercurrent of consciousness resides in us all. And we are connected.

In fact, I feel this connection with you as well. You are like me. Together we have a purpose. All of us may find different paths; however, our undercurrent is not only of our rising consciousness. It is of our unique position to be a bridge for the rational, logical-minded, left-brainers to the intuitive mind and this spirituality to which we are opening ourselves. As we said earlier in the book, we are our own unique fusion of spiritual seekers. We can explain these gifts to others like us. My calling in this moment of my journey is to get this book to you—to the linear thinkers. My most recent calling is to share words of inspiration from a guide to subsets of people like us. Different messages for different groups. I am certain my calling will keep evolving just as you will find your path to spread the word amongst our linear friends.

To some, and honestly, I see it as I reread it, what I am saying may sound a little cultish. However, it is simply sharing love, light, compassion, and kindness, and having gratitude to project positivity out into the Universe and raise the overall consciousness. We can do this even as we are working in our business clothes or while constructing a building. It is a way of being. A way to walk our individual paths.

The Presence

As we journey down this spiritual pathway, eventually we will feel "it." "It" is this feeling, this sensing, this awareness of something much bigger than us at play. Early in my journey, I remember feeling or sensing "it" during a full moon ceremony with around ten women all on this journey—and most being further along than I was. That compilation of higher-vibration individuals raised up the vibration and consciousness of the circle (including me). This is when magic can occur. This is the point where we need to throw out our thinking minds and simply be—and trust.

So what should we call this presence we feel? For those of us who still may feel like a fish out of water, there can be an uneasiness with this. *God* is likely the most recognized, but some may not feel comfortable with that idea or term. I felt a bit hypocritical using God. If I had no religious belief, how could I reference God? It has taken me these last few years to evolve to *almost* feeling comfortable. For those raised with religion, God is likely home. God is the Creator.

There is simply the awareness of something in motion bigger than us—a higher power. Maybe that is all we need to acknowledge. Yet, in our way of doing things on this planet, we find ourselves in need of a label… or is it a name? The most comfortable name that I leaned toward and still use is Great Spirit. This is the presence whom I acknowledge every morning, along with Mother Earth.

Others, and even I, can refer to the Divine. I often recite, "I surrender to Divine guidance all that is in my highest good." What does Divine mean in this context—is it a noun or an adjective? We may hear people simply state "The Divine"—making it a noun. My feeling is it is our own interpretation, since Divine mostly refers to "of God" or "God-like."

Trust me, I can be a hack when it comes to protocol and procedures, terms and phrases. I have resigned myself to knowing that if my intention is true, then my purpose is known. I am not going to offend the powers that be. "They" are patient and are happy to have us along this journey and making the effort. Likely, this is one reason why I prefer interpreting and creating my own version of spirituality.

How about Great Mystery? We may hear this term, especially within Native teachings. It is taught we are all connected to this ever-evolving, limitless consciousness. The Great Mystery is the source of all energy, of consciousness. We are all part of it. We are all one.

There are other names given by many religious traditions around the world and throughout time. There is a universal belief across traditions and throughout time that this presence exists. The beliefs have so much commonality, even in those times before worldwide communications, which make it hard to dispute the existence of this presence.

The result of many teachings is that God resides in all of us. We must only still our minds of thoughts and allow space to exist. In this space resides consciousness. This consciousness is God, is the presence.

This leads us to prayer. Creating a daily prayer ritual forges a nice connection to this spiritual world with which we are walking. Truly it is having a ritual for gratitude and intention for our day. We name or list whoever feels right to us individually, and our list may change each day. Having gratitude for the smallest of things in our life and stilling ourselves for that gratitude is powerful. It is a refreshing and pleasant addition to life.

Please, please, please do your own research as the desire strikes you. As with all of this, you are creating your own path and should not be following anyone or anything blindly. When the desire or need feels right, you will know to educate yourself on the path that is right for you. As always on this journey, no pressure. Evolve into all of this as it feels right for you. And, your way *is* the right way—for you.

Finally, for the record, I no longer roll my eyes when my mother asks me to say a prayer for someone in the family. She was raised in the church, and I know she is happy to have me finally partake from whatever authentic place I reside spiritually.

The Natural World

Throughout time Indigenous people of the world have recognized the point we made in the last section, which is *we are all one*. Indigenous cultures have long revered the natural world and had gratitude for what the natural world provided to them. Their appreciation for every aspect of nature was felt within their very being. They knew and felt that we are all one. This reverence continues within these cultures today.

While many of us are far from having that level of appreciation, the world is changing. As our planet reaches an all-time level of destruction due to the general human population's harmful behaviors and lack of reverence for the planet, the tide is beginning to turn. The Native teachings, which had been hushed for so long, are now being heard. And for those who may not follow the Native teachings, there is still a growing population who is passionately ready to protect Mother Earth.

For centuries, certain cultures have worshiped deities from the natural world. If not deities, there are spirits of the natural world who are all in motion. There is a connection between us and the natural world. We need only open ourselves to believing and trusting in the Universe. I will once again send you to watch *Avatar*!

We already dove into the need for us to have gratitude and appreciation for Mother Earth, her trees, plants, animals, and water sources. We have discussed how we can do our part in reducing our carbon footprint and being environmentally aware. We should all carry on with these practices, but since this is a chapter on Spirituality, let us talk about that aspect of nature. Let us push the believability meter a bit here.

A fun journey early on our path can be discovering our animal spirit. I do caution everyone to find a credible source to help you with this. Like many traditions, it can be Westernized, and some of the people who are "helping" us find our animal spirit have no right to be doing so. Their motives may not be pure, or they may not be properly trained. So be careful with this.

A few months after I was told what my animal spirit was, I formed a connection with it even though I thought I was projecting the ceremony into my mind. I was told we will eventually merge with our animal spirit and it will be one with us. After a few times of sensing the animal with me, I was guided to get outside and move into child pose where my spirit animal connected with me. Of course, I discredited it and truly did not believe it or tell anyone, until it happened again a year later. Same vision. Same ceremony. When I journey, meditate, or feel the need, I ask for protection from my animal spirit. I have had intuitive individuals see the animal—so there is that! As you discover your animal spirit and research its qualities, you will likely see these qualities within yourself or be inspired to incorporate these qualities into your being. Your animal spirit is there with you now—you simply may not realize it just yet.

The other is our spirit guide, typically from the bird tribe. Birds are very sacred creatures, especially in the Native traditions. These are our spiritual guides. As I entered my path, my guide placed multiple feathers at different locations in my path over one week until I finally had the nerve to pick one up—seriously! I did not want to offend anyone. I have used that feather for ceremony since then, along with two others that showed themselves soon after. I have not encountered a feather in almost three years.

There is not only our animal spirit and spirit guide, but the entire planet is full of spiritual magic. My morning prayer not only includes Mother Earth but includes all the animal spirits and the bird tribes, along with a few others for specific purposes. We need only open our senses up to taking in all these natural spirits. As we sit in nature, they will begin to show themselves.

For the last three weekends, I have had hawks circle above when I am outside doing yard work. We simply take a moment with what we witness, give gratitude, and perhaps look up the meaning. There is likely a reason for their unusual presence. We can go to the beach and sit where a rock may catch our attention. We can sit in our yard and simply pay attention to all the subtleties of nature as they pass our awareness. A couple years ago, I sat on a bluff one morning by myself and held ceremony as I was guided. Being a bit nervous about the situation, I nonetheless went into meditation. As soon as I closed my eyes, a woodpecker came within three feet of me to a tiny sapling and began pecking—audio. It allowed me to focus into meditation instantly. There are all these beautiful synchronicities available to us when we still ourselves in nature and allow ourselves to be present with the moment.

As crazy as this may sound to those of us new to or even already on this journey, nature's spirits talk to us. The volume may not be loud at this point, but we can hear them when we sit and immerse ourselves in their magic. All of us need to get out in nature more, be present with it, allow all our senses to be immersed in it, and have gratitude for all that Mother Earth provides us.

Exercises

1) Begin to sit in stillness with your eyes closed. Once again it does not have to be much time—five minutes will do. Take your seven deep breaths. Now recite, "I surrender to Divine guidance all that is in my highest good." Let yourself sit with this stillness. If you can be in nature, even better. Taking these moments helps to create a respect, a reverence, an awareness that there is something bigger than us in the Universe. Feel this power.

2) You may already be developing your morning ritual from the chapter on Self-Healing. Begin to include a moment for prayer. This is your sacred space. Include whoever or whatever you choose to include. Prayer allows you to acknowledge, give gratitude, and create an intention to begin your day. It helps create positive energy with which you can ripple outward as you step forward with your day.

3) The next time you are in a vehicle, without being a distracted driver, bring your awareness to what you can witness in nature on that drive. Make note of the river you pass over, the sun or the moon, the clouds in the sky, the birds overhead or in the trees, and the animals in the fields. If we release the thoughts that often hijack our brains as we are in our vehicles and pay attention to nature (and the road), the signs that are presented to us are extraordinary. It is like the natural world is putting on a show for us.

The intent of the Spirituality chapter was not to pit spirituality against religion, and I hope you felt that. There is room for both. There is even room for both in one person. There could be a few inner conflicts for some of us as we settle differences between beliefs of our religious tradition and new ideas brought forth on our spiritual journey, and that is okay. We will each discover the constructs of spirituality that work for us—and like everything, they will evolve over time as we do.

The intent of this chapter on Spirituality is to bring forth an awareness or create thoughts for you to consider as you make your way. I am excited for you as you define your own version of spirituality, and I am hopeful the natural world will play a part in that for you. Lastly, my advice to you as walk your path of spirituality, in whatever form it takes, is to connect to the universal consciousness through love, light, compassion, kindness, and gratitude.

Chapter Thirteen

Our Truth

Here we are! The final chapter. We are going to wrap things up with a chapter about Our Truth.

All these stepping-stones have been evolving us toward our truth. The most authentic version of ourselves. We are *creating our own, unique path on our journey toward our truest self.* As we also know, this path will continue to evolve and grow as we do during our spiritual awakening, self-awakening, and self-discovery of this journey.

Back in the Believing chapter, I told you entering the flow was the end game—where life becomes easier, brighter, simply a happier place to reside. This is true. Entering the flow is really entering the flow of consciousness. Being one with all in that flow.

As we continue our journey, we must remind ourselves that our awakening can be simply our awakening. Our awakening does not need to be more than that because by putting the truest version of ourselves out into our community, we have made a positive ripple. We have raised the universal consciousness. For those who may feel the need to take the step out into the world with our spiritual toolbox, our purpose may be to help others be that ripple. We are teaching, healing, encouraging others to step into their path and create a ripple.

What I can tell you is that making a list, racking our brain with thoughts, or even getting frustrated about what our individual purpose is on this journey is not going to give us the answers. Answers begin to arrive when we step forward with all the things we discussed in this book; give ourselves space, moments of pause; when we are present in all our moments, big and small; and when we relinquish control to the Universe. It is within these moments that the magic occurs. We find love, light, compassion, and gratitude—and answers just may begin to arrive to us.

As we walk this self-awakening path, we have already been creating a better, more sparkly, version of ourselves. We are already walking with more authenticity, integrity, love, kindness, gratitude, humility, compassion, love of self and others; and holding less judgment and less fear. These steps alone make this a path worth walking. These steps alone make us have a more positive impact on the world and contribute to raising the universal consciousness. This is our truth. This is our purpose.

But I know us. Understanding our contribution to the greater good is amazing; however, how else are we meant to contribute? What will *our* path be? We see others moving forward with more tangible contributions to the greater good. What about us? For those like me, maybe we have not added certifications or training to our spiritual toolbox. Maybe we do not feel ready to lead others in intuitive healing ceremonies. *How do we contribute?* We *stop*! We simply stop and realize things will arrive when they are meant to arrive, and we acknowledge they will continuously evolve. In the meantime, we walk our path and be a light. We are already making a difference. We need to be kind to ourselves and relinquish control to the Universe.

My newest stepping-stone arrived just recently. The magic began in 2020 while I was writing this book, in fact. Of course, life's synchronicities had already begun setting the table two years earlier—heck, five years earlier. At this point in my journey, I knew I was to write this book, and that was really all I knew. I had not quite resigned myself to the fact my intuitive gifts may be merely for myself in the comfort of my home, but I was close. Writing did not seem like an intuitive gift to me; however, it was obvious this was my path—so I trucked on. Then, on October 9, 2020, something happened that floored me! As I was getting ready to leave my home office for a bit, I walked across the room and sensed the following: "the oddity of the night." What? *That was odd,* I thought in a whisper. I walked back to my desk and wrote it down, along with the date, thinking I would sit with it later. But not the case. It came: "cannot mask…the light…that shines from within…to reveal our Soul." That was one. For the next fifteen to twenty minutes, twenty-seven of these verses came through rapidly with absolutely no thought on my part. They were written in words from the past and phrased as such too. As I came back for my forgotten mask, they resumed and then continued into the car. In all, about fifty verses came through that afternoon. When I finally asked why these messages were coming through, I received:

Feel the truth within
Write the words you feel
Understand you are a vessel
for the light that must now be

A few days later and after much more information coming through, I had to figure this out. So like many of us would do, I asked the big five questions.

Who are you?—*I am a guide. Delivered in time. Your purpose is opening, and I was called.*

What is this?—*To aid in bringing forth a message needed in these times. A voice of faith and inspiration. To be delivered to the people. To help open the door of believing in something bigger than themselves, than the world. It is time. It is time.*

Why me?—*Because it is you. You bridge the people.*

When?—*Now. We begin now.*

How?—*Write. Share. Inspire. Connect Individually. Be love. Raise them up.*

What about Book One?—*Finish. Complete. Get it out now.*

Connect Individually?—*Yes. Reach out. Get them the message. Begin with the people. One by one.*

I know, right? Trust me. I literally "told them" on day two they needed to pull back. My brain was not equipped to hear messages at this point of my journey. I cannot have voices in my head. I know I have the capacity to teeter on the edge when things occur too quickly (a fear-based reaction). And so, like how it began, I was directed to write with a wooden pencil as I transcribed the messages—no mechanical pencil…and no voices in my head. This has remained the case any time I receive. This is daily.

These messages evolved over the weeks and, of course, I have tried with all my might to determine what my purpose is to be with them. I feel strongly these are not my words. I am merely transcribing them, which lends to more of the struggle of how to appropriately share them. I adapted my website to incorporate delivering messages to people, then reversed that decision. I reached out to a few people with their individual messages, and then slowed that flow of communication. Am I supposed to put them in a book? I tried to control it! Not the answer.

In an impromptu ceremony with my sister about six weeks into this (about four days ago as I write now) and with the November 30th full moon in action, I was instructed that these words need to get out now—not in a book. As the weekend evolved, another *aha!* moment happened. Be it the original messages or new ones, I need to get them to the appropriate people. The participants of the email and social media platforms that I began earlier in the year vary by platform. Each group of people who subscribe or follow need a different message. The email addresses are all women, mostly in the forty-to-seventy age range. They will get their messages. Those who follow on Facebook and Instagram need messages of inspiration to carry on their journeys. This book is in the same vein. It is to help you find your light and inspire you to ripple outward.

And what all this comes down to is sharing the light with as many people as possible to raise the universal consciousness. It appears to be that simple. Nonetheless, let us review some of what we have learned on Our Path, let us dig into understanding Our Purpose, and end with Our Truest Self.

My hope in this chapter on Our Truth is for you to make peace in knowing that by walking an authentic path with love, kindness, compassion, and gratitude, you are already contributing to the raised universal consciousness. Discovering or uncovering your innate gift and sharing it with those around you helps to spread this positive energy and light, as well. Your individual purpose will arrive to you when it is time and will likely evolve over time, as it is a moving target. Make peace with this, be patient, and be kind to yourself. This is a journey we have all embarked upon. A journey takes time. Contribute to the greater good of a raised universal consciousness through sharing love, kindness, compassion, and gratitude in the meantime. You have that power. Be a light for others.

Our Path

Although we most certainly did not explore every possibility available for our journey, I feel like we have given ourselves a sprinkling of a lot in this book. I know you will uncover other gems that will make your journey unique to you, and I am beyond excited for you to have that opportunity.

I want you to know that there are thirteen chapters, and thus thirteen stepping-stones, in this book for a reason. The significance of the number thirteen felt important to incorporate into the book for the following personal reason, in addition to thirteen representing transformation and healing in many spiritual traditions. When I originally thought I would be sharing my *Bridget Jones* meets *Harry Potter* journal with you, it was a journal of thirteen moon lodges. And, quite literally, I held thirteen moon lodge ceremonies, a Native ceremony of bleeding into Mother Earth to honor the annual menstrual cycle of women. Not only was I guided to do this, but a handful of days after my first ceremony, I was part of an incredible full moon ceremony where I was introduced to the Rite of the Womb. It was not until six months later, having incorporated both rituals into my monthly ceremonies when I suddenly decided to research the Rite of the Womb and discovered it is the thirteenth rite of the Munay-Ki (meaning the *power of love*). This initiation was guided into existence through Marcela Lobos to bring forth a collective healing of the womb. To nurture the Rite of the Womb, which was not how it was introduced to me initially, you bleed into Mother Earth over thirteen Moon Cycles. Exactly what I had been guided to do beginning six months earlier! This may sound a little sketchy to some, but I share with you now because I am desperately learning to be unapologetic, and shedding our blood into the earth is a symbol of death and rebirth in

Native terms, as well as many other spiritual traditions—in all, it is being born to spirit. And this journey has been nothing less than a death and rebirth for me.

A quote from Ohky Simine Forest from *Dreaming the Council Ways* (2009): "*...the genuine sacrifice of the blood of your spirit imbues you with a tremendous sense of connectedness, higher purpose, and a great inner serenity throughout all the challenges on your path.*"

I offer you this information because I want you to be open to things that may make you feel uncomfortable, awkward, and even crazy at times—literally crazy. Even though I held this ritual by myself, engaging in such a ceremony for thirteen moon cycles was so far outside of my being and comfort zone, let alone sharing with anyone the fact I was holding such rituals—yet I did it...even in the winter months. I felt it was necessary. I did not choose it. It came to me. These nontraditional (in our view) things, practices, events can come forward on our paths. They come for a reason. As long as they feel safe and intuitively sound, be open.

For those who are curious about such a ceremony, there is this. First, I am not suggesting you follow my lead in bleeding into Mother Earth, as I do not suggest you follow anyone blindly. If you choose to partake in such a ceremony, you are doing so as an act of free will and agree to do your own research. Okay, legally covered! Bleeding into Mother Earth can be a simple symbolic gesture regardless of your gender identity, or you can offer actual blood if that is what you want to do and are comfortable with doing so. What I have discovered on my journey and I will share with you here is often our intent or willingness to offer, partake in, have gratitude toward, pray for, or offer a thought—all with intention—can be enough. Nothing has to be perfect. If our intent is true, a symbolic gesture or offering is fine. If our intent is true, a ceremony can last a few minutes rather than an hour. If our intent is true, we are being heard.

This path toward our truest self with a goal of helping to raise the universal consciousness is about becoming that authentic person we mentioned at the start of the chapter. Many of the stepping-stones we covered in this book give us a place to unload some baggage so we may step forward in that light as our authentic selves. Sometimes we may get a little dirty. The analogy I offer here is for you to think about cleaning out a closet or cupboard. We often spread out all the contents on the floor or table and go through them piece by piece to see what stays, what gets recycled, and what needs to leave the space altogether. Eventually, we can take what remains and return the items back to their places. During this awakening journey, we are going to do this with what is inside of us, along with the people, places, and things in our lives.

So without recapping chapter by chapter here, I hope you will all discover which stepping-stones speak to you for your unique path toward your truest self. It is a journey and takes time, but each step toward our authentic self allows our light to shine a little more brightly each day.

Our Purpose

By choosing to walk in the light with love, kindness, compassion, and gratitude, we are already fulfilling our purpose. We should all make certain to understand this aspect of our awakening. It can be that simple. Nonetheless, let us deepen our understanding of this path a bit more.

There is contributing to the greater good of raising the universal consciousness and this is the same for everyone. It is our impetus, our driving force. And then there is our individual calling, which further supports the raised universal consciousness. The Holy Grail we all seem to be searching to uncover for ourselves.

Let us begin with the raised universal consciousness. We have mentioned this purpose throughout the book, but I want to take you on a more in-depth journey with it. About a month before I finished writing the first draft of this book, understanding the true essence of being one with all hit me over the head. There may be people out there who wonder how this could be such a shocking revelation for me. I mean, I knew the phrase and thought I understood the concept, but I truly did not. Perhaps I was not ready prior to this. Maybe I was not quite ready to grasp this concept of being one with all and how it relates to the raised universal consciousness.

Since it was such a critical piece for me, let us hammer it home for us all in terms I wish I had understood earlier. This consciousness thing. It is energy. We are all energy—currently within our human bodies, but always in spirit. Everything is energy. So if our objective is to raise consciousness, how do we do it? We begin within ourselves and stepping forward on our path. The result is we are walking with more authenticity, integrity, love, kindness, gratitude, humility, compassion, love of self and others, and holding less judgment and less fear, as I mentioned earlier in the chapter. In simply becoming this truest version of ourselves, we ripple outward this positivity, this positive energy, which in turn raises the universal consciousness. Now take a deep breath for the next part— do it, please. This limitless existence of energy...or consciousness, this is the Higher Being, God, Great Spirit, whatever you may want to call it. By us feeding into it, we are part of it—it is part of us. We all have this consciousness within us. Which means...God, Great Spirit, the Presence, a Higher Being is within each and every one of us. What? This is why and how we will read from a variety of sources and multiple traditions across continents and over time that we are *one with all*.

Think of an ocean wave. We are the wave. When we recede, we still exist as part of the larger ocean. This is us and consciousness. I cannot take credit for this analogy. I have heard it a number of times in a variety of ways and paraphrase it here.

Okay, how does our positivity raise the consciousness? Being energy, it does not go away; however, it can change. Think of how we feel when a negative person is in our space. We want to remove ourselves, right? I remember one day when I was feeling a bit angsty and thought I was doing a great job of masking it in front of my then nine-year-old son. Being my empathic sponge, he entered the room and was overcome by my emotions, which I thought were contained inside of me. On the other end of the spectrum, think how we feel when we are around someone who shines. It lifts us up. Music, movies, news, Black Friday shopping— all of these can influence our energy, good and bad. Whether we fully believe his study or not, look up Masaru Emoto, who studied how water crystals can change shape based on the positive or negative intentions around them. It is quite fascinating. So by being positive energy ourselves and by exposing others to our positive energy, one by one we can help to raise the universal consciousness—which is God, Great Spirit, The Divine, the Higher Being, the Presence we feel…which is also us!

Phew. Now we know and understand, and maybe believe, all of this. Still, what about our individual calling to further support raising the universal consciousness? This is where we get to leave our personal touch, right? Is it as simple as choosing a major and discovering how we may be able to further support raising the universal consciousness? Not a chance! This is the place where we stop, we still, and we relinquish control. This is where we breathe. Seriously.

If we really stop for a moment, we will realize that our desperate need to know our individual purpose is merely our ego getting involved. Do not be hard on yourself, we all do it. Even if we get "the answer" of our individual calling, we are going to continue to evolve over time. The "answer" today is a stepping-stone for tomorrow's purpose, and so on. The finish line will continue to move. So when we place a tool in our spiritual toolbox, we may exclaim to ourselves and to our tribe, "I believe I discovered my purpose!" When the truth is, we are simply stepping forward in supporting the raised universal consciousness— we are evolving. We are continuing along our path and will likely have another stepping-stone placed in front of us before long. This is our journey. Getting this book published is my calling today, but I know it is merely a stepping-stone toward an undefined end. We continue to move forward, we trust, and we relinquish control to the Universe. My next stepping-stones are beginning to show themselves as I near completion of this book. Do I know my end purpose? Not a chance. Making peace with this unknown is easier said than done; however, making peace is what will bring us our inner peace as we enter the flow.

I am guessing many of you reading this book have been on the expectations route since you were in elementary school. This journey is often about stepping off that preset plan to create our own, unique path, but awakening does not have to derail everything about our journey up to this point. Awakening and contributing to the universal consciousness has the full potential to act as a complement to whatever career path we are currently on if that is our passion. Think of a teacher, a nurse, a retailer, a doctor, a restaurant worker, and the like, and think of how many people those professions have contact with each workday. Those of us in such professions have a tremendous opportunity to positively impact other people. Our ripple opportunity is exponential! This may be our calling, or a stepping-stone of our purpose, to further contribute to raising the universal consciousness.

For those who do not feel the passion for our current jobs or careers, we are the ones who may struggle most with *how do I further contribute?* We should continue to remind ourselves that being a contributor toward raising the universal consciousness can still occur while we are following the path of our individual purpose. This is because the goal of raising the universal consciousness must be the drive behind this journey we are on—be it in discovering our calling or within our career. Without living in that light, likely we will always be searching.

Now for honesty. I am currently following the stepping-stones that have been presented to me on my purposeful path—between this book and the new messages coming through. Do I feel like I am still figuring it out? Yes. Do I get paid for my new path yet? No. Does that leap of faith add stress at times? Yes. Do I try to trust that it will all work itself out? Yes. Do I still have angst that I am writing this book, trying to build a platform, and trying to get messages out to people while my "work" heads to the backseat a bit? Yes. Do I feel incredibly thankful I have had the opportunity to shift my focus as I have during this pandemic? Yes. Can I maintain this focus shift long-term not knowing the end result? I do not know.

We have talked a lot about what speaks to each of us throughout this book. No time more so than here. Each of our paths will call to us over time. We all need to attempt to take the pressure off ourselves. Take the pressure off our ingrained thinking that we need to succeed at this. For what does that even mean? This is a different beast than what many of us are used to tackling. This is not a corporate ladder. We all need to focus on contributing to the raised universal consciousness. Be authentic, kind, loving, compassionate, grateful people. Be present in our lives and our individual calling will begin to arrive when it is meant to arrive and will evolve as it is meant to evolve. Be patient and be kind to ourselves.

Our Truest Self

Throughout the book, we have said we are *creating our own, unique path on our journey toward our truest self.* What exactly, who exactly is our truest self? My interpretation of our truest self includes authenticity, who we are when everything is stripped away, along with love, light, compassion, kindness, and gratitude.

When we mix these qualities in the pot, we are able to contribute to the greater good of a raised universal consciousness, we have discovered our place in that purpose, and we do this all from a place of genuine truth in who we are. Now, with that said, we also know we evolve. Perhaps this is why we say, *toward our truest self.*

There is a lot for us to do to be the truest version of ourselves. Luckily, it is a journey, which means it happens over time. We have learned a multitude of things along our path—from Filling Our Canoe to how we can use Crystals and Stones. We have tested our Believability and dipped our toe into Spirituality. We have learned the importance of living In the Present moment, along with the importance of caring for ourselves and giving ourselves space. We know we all need to take care of Mother Earth, as Mother Earth takes care of us.

In walking this path, our light switch is already on. Perhaps we are initially on a dimmer switch; however, each and every day we walk this path, our light becomes brighter.

Soon after the initial round of messages came through to me in October of 2020, I began receiving messages for individuals. Before long, I received a general message for everyone. A clear call to action for us all.

These messages come to remind you all
that your actions can create change in positive ways.
Embrace your message. You all have a gift that needs
to be shared. Each day you should ask of yourself what
you have done to share your gift today.

The above message was explained as it is going to take all of us to right the ship. That we each have a gift or gifts that need to be shared at this time.

Some of the individual messages were simply about a person's light or kindness or smile. Another message was about a person's charitable contributions, while another was teaching people to dream. There was a message encouraging one person to simply allow her energy to be felt. There were messages of telling stories with photographs and telling others' stories with words, along with writing lyrics needing to be heard by the world. The list goes on.

This left me thinking that between aiding in raising the universal consciousness and discovering our individual purpose, there is sharing our gifts. I also believe our gifts are more closely related to our authenticity. They often come from within our being. A person whose smile lights up a room is born with that gift. So as we project our light, love, compassion, and gratitude into the world to aid in raising the universal consciousness, and we work on relinquishing control to discover the path of our individual calling, we have our gifts with which we can use to be that light for others. And then we ask ourselves, "What have we done to share our gift today?"

As we *create our own, unique path on our journey toward our truest self*, let us embody the confidence to step forward into the world as that truest version of ourselves. Our growing lights may attract some critical moths, but they are not our concern. We know our intent is pure. We know we are here to make a difference. We know our truth.

Exercises

1) As we discussed quite a bit in this book, I recommend you simply choose a couple of suggestions or examples from the stepping-stones that may have jumped out to you and give focus to them to begin or continue forward on your path. Emitting positive energy out into the world is essential, yet it must come from an authentic place, and to do that, we must do a little housekeeping of our mind, body, and spirit as well.

2) Practice embodying positive energy. Once again, be with it—as always nature is a great place for this. Think about each of the following words

individually, what they mean to you, and what they feel like to both give and to receive them: love, kindness, compassion, and gratitude. Allow yourself to feel the power in them. Stand tall with them and open your heart space. A great addition to this practice is to stand in tree pose (or your interpretation of the pose) while out in nature.

3) What is your gift—not your individual purpose, but your gift? What is the gift with which you were born? You know what it is. Slow for a moment. People have recognized it within you even if you have not. Is it your energy when you walk into the room? Is it your smile? Is it your voice? Is it your courage? Share your gift with others. The world needs to see, hear, feel, touch what you have to share. What have you done to share your gift today? Ask this of yourself every day!

Congratulations and thank you for completing this book! I will be forever grateful to all of you for sending me your unseen messages of the need for this book in our linear corner of the world.

There is a lot to digest, and I am right there with you. There is an immense amount of information available to us from every corner of the spiritual world. Each time we absorb information or experiences, they have the ability to alter our interpretation, our path, our trajectory. Although the unstructured aspect of the path can make us feel a bit out of control, I think this is fascinating to us as well. Our journey is truly for each of us to create.

The stones we choose to place on our path are the building blocks to the new version of ourselves. Building this new version of ourselves is going to give us the capacity to begin emitting our positive energy out into the Universe and to ripple through our communities. And we will continue to have patience as our individual calling unfolds, taking us on a journey with no defined destination other than to further support the raised universal consciousness in a way unique only to us. In the meantime, we share our gifts with the world and be a light for others— as we *create our own, unique path on our journey toward our truest self.*

Much love, light, compassion, and gratitude to you all.

Acknowledgments

This book was in a cocoon for much of its life. No one saw it and only a few people knew of its potential future existence. But once again, the people I love most in my life have taught me that when I let them inside my world, when I allow the light into the cocoon, transformation and magic ensue.

When I gathered up the courage to tell my children, Sam and Cooper, and my partner, Tom, that I was writing a book, their unwavering support and encouragement gave me the confidence to pursue this project. I love them for many reasons, but this support brought a new level of love. Every day I learn from each of them.

My parents provide unconditional love and support regardless of what I do in life and this journey, along with the book, has been no different. I am grateful for the safe foundation they have always provided and knowing they stand with me in whatever I choose to tackle in life.

My sister, Michelle, is not only a supportive family member through the writing of this book. She is one of the two people who brought me onto the spiritual journey. Together we have participated in more clearings, rituals, ceremonies, and healings than I have with anyone else. We have shed many tears, some good and some more difficult—but all necessary, on this journey together over the last six years. I will be forever grateful for the beautiful moments we have shared and the paths to which they have brought us.

My friend, Jen, is the second person, along with Michelle, who started me on this journey of self-awakening. Without their guidance and friendship, I would be in a far different place than now. Jen saw this book when it was just a sparkle in my eye and has been one of my biggest champions in bringing it to reality. I am beyond grateful for her friendship, love, and support.

My shaman, Ryan, is my spiritual mentor. Many of the things I have written about in this book were brought into my life through Ryan. His guidance over the last four years has allowed me to step forward as my truest self. He has helped me nurture this book from concept to creation to completion. Encouraging me all the way—with nudges when necessary. When I told him the title of the book, he simply said, "I have known it my whole life."

About the time I began the journey that gave me the content to write this book, a whole additional family was added to my life as well. Little did I know that four wise women would enter my world and bring such love with them. I am so grateful for the Kendrick ladies and the support and encouragement they provide—each in their unique way.

To all the magical people who have crossed my path, are currently on my path, and will be on my path someday, I thank you. There are so many of you who have left your mark on me, and I am grateful to have every one of you in my life.

Over the year of writing and editing this final version of the book, I began an online platform and as I have tentatively shared snippets of this book and my journey, I am humbled by the people who have shown support. Some of you I have known for years, and others are new names to me. I thank you all for your support. It has been amazing.

Finally, to the folks of Maine Authors Publishing, I thank you for giving self-publishing authors a welcoming home and cooperative option for publishing our work. A special thank you to Christina for being my guide through this unknown world of publishing and providing understanding and kindness when needed. An enormous thank you to my editor, Jennifer, for cleaning up my writing, reminding me of the rules of grammar in the process, and teaching me the difference between a dash and a hyphen, as well as to Dan for facilitating my editing needs

Acknowledgments

and stepping in when necessary. Much gratitude to my graphic designer, Michelle, for her patience and positive nature as she walked me through the cover and interior design process—transforming my manuscript into this book.

References & Suggested Reading & Viewing

Adamson, Andrew, and Vicky Jenson, directors. 2001. *Shrek*. DreamWorks Distribution.

Asprey, David. *Fast This Way: Burn Fat, Heal Inflammation, and Eat Like the High-Performing Human You were Meant to Be.* New York: Harper Wave, 2021.

Bailey, Frazer. *E-motion 2.0.* Passion River Productions, 2014.

Bardugo, Leigh. *Ruin and Rising.* New York: Henry Holt and Company, 2014.

Bündchen, Gisele. *Lessons: My Path to a Meaningful Life.* New York: Avery, 2018.

Cameron, James, director. 2009. *Avatar.* Twentieth Century Fox.

Carey, Ken. *Return of the Bird Tribes.* New York: HarperOne, 1988.

Forest, Ohky Simine. *Dreaming the Council Ways: True Native Teachings from the Red Lodge.* York Beach, ME: Samuel Weiser, Inc., 2000.

Fuchs, Natalie. *The Enlightenment*. Leelame Productions in association with MCDLR Production, 2017.

Gibran, Kahlil. *The Prophet*. New York: Knopf, 1995.

Meadows, Kenneth. *The Medicine Way: A Shamanic Path to Self-Mastery*. Rockport, MA: Element Books, Inc., 1990.

Nestor, James. *Breath: The New Science of a Lost Art*. New York: Riverhead Books, 2020.

Ober, Clinton, Stephen T. Sinatra, and Martin Zucker. *Earthing: The Most Important Health Discovery Ever!* Columbus, OH: Basic Health Publications, Inc., 2010.

Pond, David. *Chakras for Beginners: A Guide to Balancing Your Chakra Energies*. Woodbury, MN: Llewellyn Publications, 1999.

Puddicombe, Andy. *The Headspace Guide to Meditation & Mindfulness: How Mindfulness Can Change Your Life in Ten Minutes s Day*. New York: St. Martin's Press, 2011.

Sams, Jamie. *Dancing the Dream: The Seven Sacred Paths of Human Transformation*. New York: HarperCollins Publishers, 1998.

Tickell, Josh and Rebecca, directors. 2019. *The Earthing Movie: The Remarkable Science of Grounding*. Big Picture Ranch.

Tolle, Eckhart. *A New Earth: Awakening to Your Life's Purpose*. New York: Penguin Books, 2005, 2016.

Turk, Jon. *The Raven's Gift: A Scientist, a Shaman, and Their Remarkable Journey Through the Siberian Wilderness*. New York: St. Martin's Press, 2010.

Van Sant, Gus, director. 1997. *Good Will Hunting*. Miramax.

Villoldo, Alberto. *Shaman, Healer, Sage: How to Heal Yourself and Others with the Energy Medicine of the Americas*. New York: Harmony Books, 2000.